A GOOD DIVORCE
BEGINS HERE

A Guide to Surviving and Thriving Afterward

TOM STURGES

NEWMAN SPRINGS PUBLISHING
320 Broad Street
Red Bank, NJ 07701

First originally published by Newman Springs Publishing 2021

A Paradiso Press Book

Cover design by Danielle Stein

ISBN 978-1-63692-998-9 (Paperback)
ISBN 978-1-63692-999-6 (Digital)

Printed in the United States of America

CONTENTS

FOREWORD

When someone comes to me and says that he or she wants a divorce, the first questions I ask are these: Have you tried your best to keep the marriage together? Have you and your spouse gone to counseling? Have you done all you can to make it work? And when it is clear that the couple have tried everything or chose not to try everything because they were convinced that nothing really could save the marriage, I then proceed to represent my client, whether man or woman, in securing the divorce.

I have never, in fifty-plus years of private law practice, asked a client if they wanted a "good" divorce. It's not something I was taught in my domestic relations classes in law school, nor was it something I ever even thought about. In the end, many of the hundreds of divorces I have handled turned out to be good, and a much smaller number turned out to be "bad," but those are subjective terms, and the results of the process are very much in the eyes of the beholder.

In *A Good Divorce Begins Here*, Tom Sturges takes the subjectivity out of it completely. He gives readers a road map to a good divorce. I recommend this book to every man or woman contemplating divorce or facing an unwanted divorce. It should be read by anyone and everyone. There are so many important subjects to consider when one is about to take this major step in life, and Tom covers them in great detail with sound and thoughtful advice.

I like to say, As you go through life, make *this* your goal: watch the donut, not the hole. This means that when you start anything, make sure you know what you want to accomplish and how you want to accomplish it. As you read all that Tom Sturges has written, you will start to understand the undeniable need for a good divorce, not only for yourself but for your spouse, your children, and your future. Tom states—and I agree completely—that the three most important ingredients in the recipe for a good divorce are: kindness, respect, and generosity. Easy to say but not so easy to achieve, especially in the most difficult days of the process and the moments that can easily overwhelm.

This book will go a long way in helping you understand what you need to do to achieve a good divorce and have a good life afterward.

Michael J. Schiff, JD, attorney at law

INTRODUCTION

My father was married four times, my mother three. Even my oldest brother had three marriages.

So I was absolutely determined that I would only get married once, and no divorce. Then life happened. With it came homes, mortgages, children, debt. Getting fired, getting hired. Successes and failures. A miscarriage. Two funerals coming too soon. And then, suddenly somehow, I was in the middle of a divorce. Out of the blue it seemed.

Two clear choices were before me: Let it the worst thing that ever happened, or try to make it one of the best. I chose to try and make it one of the best. I chose kindness, respect, and generosity. I tried to be gracious, and silent, and stay friends with all our friends and stay close with everyone in her family. My mom really loved my first wife and I didn't want that to change either.

At the end of the day, with just a couple of little bumps in the road, it worked. It was a good divorce, for both of us. Nobody is angry or resentful, there is no lingering animus. We live two blocks apart and talk all the time. As you will read, her brother saved my life and her mom is my real estate broker.

All that to say your divorce does not have to be something awful. It does not have to break you, spiritually or otherwise. It doesn't have to be the end of everything you knew. Your marriage can just come to an end, if you want it to end. Even if it's not your choice, it is your option.

This book is my take on how to make that happen.

Tom Sturges
Los Angeles, California
tomsturges.net

CHAPTER 1

The Beginning of the End

Thinking About It

You are at this point because you have thought it over, and you think it's over. Something went down, and that was it, the last straw. And for however many reasons, you have now decided that it is time to move on. In many marriages, especially ones that need a little work, seeds of doubt soon bloom into roses of certainty. It can happen almost overnight. Just a few years ago, you two were on some island beach, sipping colorful drinks and wiling away hour after hour. But now you're looking at the person of your dreams with a different point of view. Maybe a little less friendly and not quite as romantic. No doubt both of you have changed since you got together.

But before you start checking the Internet for a new place, hold up there just one quick second. As bad as it is to get something *started* too soon, *it is even worse to try to end something too soon.* Particularly a marriage. Are you sure that divorce is the absolutely right step to take? Are you certain that all other options have been considered carefully and then dismissed beforehand? Are you letting a very important decision like this one take its time getting made, or are you rushing to make it yourself? While immediate happiness and long-awaited relief is important, these are not the only important things you are dealing with.

Or possibly you are looking down the barrel of an unwanted divorce. The shoe is on the other foot, and it is your spouse who has decided that he or she has had enough and wants more out of the rest of their life than you can provide. Through no fault of your own, the marriage you were counting on is about to slip through your fingers. Either way, the steps to follow are the same, provided you want to enjoy the many benefits of a good divorce.

Successful relationships are very rare, and the statistics on divorce back this up completely. As of 2019, nearly *half* of all marriages in the United States ended in divorce. That's a 50 percent failure rate. Which means all those people went to the trouble of finding someone, dating, getting engaged, getting married, having kids and buying a house, and then trying to keep it all together—for what? They risked all that time and treasure on a fifty-fifty proposition? They went to all that trouble and turmoil for a coin flip? It's like they took their life savings and went to Las Vegas, walked up to the roulette wheel at the Hard Rock Hotel, and bet it all on red. And so did you. And so do all of us who get married. We take that same chance with those same odds.

With that thought in mind, please consider the possibility that getting a divorce should be the last step you take and only after several other steps have been tried and taken. Maybe this is not what you want to think about, especially if you're angry and looking for solace, or your wife or husband is just as angry and wants theirs, but it's what you both *have* to consider. Explore every single chance you have before giving up on the relationship.

For instance:

1. Share every aspect of your feelings and hold nothing back. Discuss everything and anything you are going through. And explore every option on the table. Repeat: *Hold Nothing Back.*
2. Bring in the right therapist to help make these conversations work for both of you. *Right* is the key. The wrong one will just take your money and make things worse (as discussed later).
3. Move to another room or bedroom in your house before you pack up and move *out* of your house. It is much harder to move back in from a new apartment than it is to return to your bed from the living room.
4. If religion or faith is one of the ties that bind you and your spouse, bring this force to bear on your relationship by praying on it and seeking the counsel of your elders and mentors.
5. Share the details of your secret heart and its sadness with some of your best pals and let them provide ears and guidance to you. You will be surprised how much your friends know about you if you just ask them.

If there is any chance at all that you can turn things around before opting for divorce, try your hardest to do so. If you do finally end up in a divorce, *it will likely be a better divorce if you both gave the marriage every single opportunity to succeed.* Your soon-to-be-ex will appreciate and respect that you tried everything to make it work between you. This will lead you both to a better ending and, more than likely, a better relationship going forward. Maybe even friendship. At this point, you may not care about having a better relationship, but that will likely change, especially if there are children in the mix.

Many people make their biggest decisions, especially the really big ones, in moments of extreme emotion. In anger or jealousy, or sometimes even while in ecstasy. And that's fine if the decision is about a new car or a watch. But divorce is one of those decisions that should be carefully considered before any action is taken. There is plenty of time. And there are a lot of things to consider. Before you race to start a divorce, try to think the whole thing through and more than once. Keep evaluating the situation you are in now and the one you're going to be in. Reach a decision, don't race to one. Most decisions will make themselves very clear if you give them enough time.

A man I know did not handle the early stages of his divorce well at all. He made the decision that his marriage was over while he was thousands of miles from home, in bed with his girlfriend. Talk about a bad time to be thinking about such important things! And while he was busy planning the next stage of his life, his wife hired a programmer to bypass his flimsy computer passwords. His life was hacked and cracked wide open. Like a walnut. Exposed were all the secrets and lies his meandering heart had failed to share. Including the purchase of a property in another country, the hiding of funds in new bank accounts, the rewriting of his will, and so on.

When she learned what he had been plotting behind her back, the wife almost lost her mind. Well, actually she *did* lose her mind and hasn't been the same since. When he got home from his "business trip," all his expensive suits, shirts, ties, and shoes were piled in the front yard, getting soaked by the sprinklers. Locks were changed, papers filed, the children were on notice.

The divorce was a bloodbath, and the ex-husband and ex-wife still don't speak. Messages are passed between them via intermediaries. Friends divided into his and hers instantly and were very vocal about why. It did not have to be this way, and every day he knows this better and better. Instead of a pleasant farewell with some well-earned tears on both sides, his divorce was a skinning. He walked into the courtroom a liar, a fraud, and a cheat. The judge had little or no sympathy. They had been married for twenty years or so and had children and homes and property, and promises made in earnest. She got everything she wanted. He got very little that he wanted. What he should have done was come clean with his wife, told her he was unhappy and why, and then tried to make it better. Had he handled things differently, his wife would have known that he treated her fairly and honestly. She would likely have treated him the same way in the divorce. Just a modicum of respect would have gone a long way. You do not have to let his story become your story.

As you are considering divorce as an option, whether it is your choice or it is being forced upon you, make sure there are plenty of good reasons to end your marriage before you end it. Make sure you have given the relationship every possible chance to succeed before you declare it a failure. Make sure you have spoken with lots of people about it and sought their counsel and wisdom. Then if you still need to leave, do it honestly and honorably and respectfully. This is the key to a good divorce. Respect the ex from the moment the process begins.

Questions to Ask Yourself

1. Have you given this relationship every chance to survive, and still there is nothing left to stay for and nothing left to love for?
2. Is the reason you're thinking about leaving this relationship really a good-enough reason to leave this person forever?
3. Is the love affair really and truly over? Is there absolutely no hope? Is there zero chance you can work this rough patch out? Is there nothing at all left to fight for?
4. Is your spouse still in love with you? Yes, this is a very personal question for a book to ask its reader, especially since there is no way to check your answer. But nonetheless, it is the question only you can answer.
5. Does your spouse still thrill at your arrival? Still laugh at a joke heard four hundred times? Look for you in crowds and smile when your eyes meet?
6. Does your spouse still welcome you into bed on a regular basis?
7. Is your spouse *still* into you and the marriage?

If the answer is yes to any of these questions, especially 4 and 6, then your relationship is still alive and still has a chance to survive. And you may be acting the fool if you are thinking of divorcing. Never leave a loving heart. It is a bad move. If your spouse is still in love with you, keep trying to make the relationship work. Do not walk out. Give it more. Give it your best. Give it your all. Brigitte Bardot famously said, "When I love, I do it without counting. I give myself entirely. And each time it is the grandest love of my life." I cannot say if this is true for all women, but let's assume it might be. Meaning that if the Brigitte Bardot in your life is still all about you, you cannot walk out. Or if you are the Brigitte Bardot, you have to keep trying until there is no doubt, just certainty. A few weeks or months of discussing and considering is nothing compared to the years that will stretch out after this decision is finally made.

8. Did you happen to notice when you found yourself so unhappy that divorce seemed like a good idea? Can you trace it back to a specific day? What is something someone said? Or did?

9. Did there happen to be a major event in your life that knocked you on your heels, that left you to wonder and worry about the amount of time you have left? Maybe health related? A life change in other words?

10. Did you witness some exchange between your spouse and someone that gave rise to a sudden and terrible jealousy? And now you cannot figure out how to get out of it?

These are the kinds of questions you need to ask yourself. These are the kinds of things you need to consider. If you decide in the end that the marriage is truly over, you will have set the stage for a good divorce by giving the marriage every chance to succeed.

Good Reasons to End Bad Marriages

Sometimes there is no other course but to pack it up and walk. For everyone in a relationship, the reasons might be very different, but there are some basic thresholds that to me are unforgivable.

1. You discover that your spouse has had a long-standing affair. Not a quick mistake at an industry convention. Somehow that might be forgiven. But think along the lines of Prince Charles and Camilla Parker Bowles, or Laura Linney in *Ozark*. Like it's very regular with the other person and there's a toothbrush and clean underwear at the house. Two words: *See ya!* Two words for the other person: *Thank You!*

2. You realize, quite sadly, that you are not in love with your husband or wife anymore and unlikely to ever be again. In some arranged marriages, there was never any "in love" to begin with, so excluding those situations, if there's no love, there's almost no point in continuing the battle.

3. You finally see the light, and it shines on the fact that your spouse is actually not in any way your soul mate and maybe never was. Maybe you got

20

a little mixed up during that first year of constant attraction. Hot, yes. Everyone understands this delusion. Soul*ful*, yes. Again it might have been all the alcohol and trips to Vegas. But your soul mate? The person you want to spend the rest of your life with and have children with and put up with everything they do and might do and all that? It's a high bar. And if your husband or wife doesn't reach it, get out. Now. Before it's too late. Like before too much more of your life slips by.

4.   You start to feel like Detective Columbo because your husband is very clearly not who he said he was when you guys were just dating. And now the lies just keep on coming. His dad was *not* an ambassador? He just *worked* at the Ambassador Hotel? His uncle is actually *in* prison, not a guard *at* a prison? In my view, one little lie is forgivable. Thirty little ones are not at all.

5.   You have become a victim of violence. Any violence of any kind, whether physical, spiritual, emotional, or otherwise, is completely and totally unacceptable. It's a shame to even consider this kind of thing, but violence is a neon sign that you are in the wrong relationship and possibly a very bad marriage. Nobody hits just once.

6.   An aggravating personal trait or habit that has finally revealed itself, and you know that you cannot and will not survive its presence in your life. You find yourself cringing at the possibility that it will happen again, knowing that it will, and

maybe soon. This would include finding out that your spouse is a screamer for instance. Or a raging alcoholic. Or a thief. Or has the makings of a coke addict. These kinds of traits are unchangeable without years of therapy and persistent attention, and the person who comes out the other end is going to be nothing like the one you fell in love with anyway. So let them get drunk and scream at someone else. You, hit the highway.

The Right Therapist, Not Just Any Therapist

I ran into a friend who was getting a divorce. He had already moved out of his house and moved in with his yoga instructor. He had already set his family on the traditional course of mayhem and disintegration. He had already started to walk blindly into a future full of his/hers, lawyers' bills, and years of sadness. Talking to him was actually one of the inspirations for this book, namely me thinking I could share some of the things I did right with other people who were doing things wrong. But not in time for him, unfortunately.

He described the process of divorce as one of the worst things that ever happened to him. He was losing his home. Most of the friends were going with her instead of him. His kids were turning against him too, and on and on it went. He had to start his life over, and it really didn't have to be this way. It didn't have to end like that. Up until the last few moments, he was willing to keep trying. He did not want to leave everything he had going. He and his wife sought the counsel of a therapist, and that turned out to be the worst mistake of all. He was willing and happy to go to therapy to work things out, but he and his wife made the mistake of choosing the wrong therapist.

Ultimately the downward spiral caused by talking with the wrong person doomed his chances and set in motion a series of events that have cost him pretty much everything he loved.

Here's what happened. He and his wife were in therapy, in couple's therapy. They were still talking and still living together but, by going to a therapist, were acknowledging that something was not working. The therapist focused on their communication and tried to help them mainly in that area. They went for a couple of months to see the therapist, and when they got started, the therapist would say to the wife, "Do you have anything to say to your husband?"

For the next few minutes, the wife would regale him with issues, some of them going back to the very first years of their marriage twenty years earlier. He remembers the therapist—also a woman—nodding her head and encouraging the wife to go on and go on. So his wife did exactly that, bearing all his sins and foibles, leaving them out there for all to see.

When she was finished, the therapist would say to my friend, "How about you?"

Since he was the kind of guy who didn't hold on to his resentments all that well and was quick to overlook the bad in exchange for viewing the good, he would say that he had no complaints. And it went on this way for months. Ultimately these conversations sealed the fate of the marriage and sent it over the edge.

Despite the fact that it was supposed to be couples therapy, the therapist only helped the wife. And at a certain point, it was like there were two women ripping him apart. After the sessions, the wife was still just as angry and just as vitriolic as when she walked in. Rehashing old news got her really steamed up, and there was no calming her down.

This was all overwhelming for my friend, who was unable to defend himself or right the ship. What should have helped his marriage actually accelerated its demise. He had tried to do the right thing, but when he reached for a life preserver, all he had in his hands was a snake. Instead of effecting a rescue, the therapist was like a fireman who arrives at a smoldering house with a can of gas and some matches.

I asked him what he thought he could have done differently to avoid, or at least diminish, the terrible things that were happening to him. He said this, "We tried to do the right thing, but we had the wrong therapist. She was not helping us. She was hurting us. She bonded with my wife and not me."

Oh, ouch! Since nothing unites two people like a common enemy, my friend became that common enemy of the wife and the therapist. They became closer, pushing him right out. I suspect they might still be friends, but that's just cynical me.

Maybe, like my friend, you have reached out to an outside source to help you. If you have chosen to bring in a therapist, and if your instinct tells you this therapist is not helping you and is not the right person for you and this relationship, then stop it. Trust your instinct and find another one, find the one who wants you to stay together, not the one who is just as content to help you split apart. My friend was trying to do the right thing, trying with all his might and all his efforts. And he got completely screwed. He was trying to keep the ball in the air, but he chose the wrong person to help. He should have recognized, much earlier on, that she was killing any chances of reconciliation and found someone who could. Her force ended a relationship that maybe shouldn't have ended.

If your marriage is struggling, the right therapist can be your salvation. The wrong one can be your ruin. At that moment, the *right* therapist is everything, but not just *any* therapist. Make sure you choose the one best for you and your life, you and your spouse, you and your marriage.

Talk Before You Walk

The last few days of a marriage are very sad days. All the family photos just remind you of what was, no longer a symbol of what is. The memories that assail your heart will feel like ridicule instead of acknowledgment. You may be walking through your house, as your house, for the last time.

But hold on. While it may be on life support, or the equivalent of relationship intensive care, your marriage is still alive. It still has possibilities. It still has a chance, and saving it is still an option, there within your reach, if you still care enough to try and make something good happen. So whatever else you do, keep on talking. And keep on listening. Be honest with each other about what has happened and why. Forgive and forget as much as you can bear to do. Keep identifying the dreams you had together and still have together. Those dreams are the bridge to your future, whether it is you together with your spouse, moving forward, or friends someday after the divorce is final. Don't assume it's over just because it feels that way. Be certain you both want it to end. And if there's a chance to relight the flame, talk yourself into it and give it one more conversation.

What Your Spouse Might Be Thinking

During both my marriages I worked in the music business, mostly in music publishing. One of my responsibilities was to find unrecorded songs and give them to artists who could sing them and bring them to life (see appendix 1 for a list of some of them). Altogether I found homes for eighty-plus songs. One of them really stands out as I write this book. It is a song that describes what the last moments of a love affair are like. It was recorded by Celine Dion and produced by Christopher Neil and Aldo Nova, written by Peter Sinfield and my writer Andy Hill. After its release, the song became one of Ms. Dion's biggest hits and reached number 1 all over Europe and number 2 in the United States. I'm proud to have been part of it. I am including the lyrics here as a glimpse into what your spouse might be thinking as you approach the final days of your marriage. And also to say that the marriage isn't over until you both say it is.

Think Twice

By Andy Hill and Pete Sinfield

Don't think I can't feel that there's something wrong
You've been the sweetest part of my life for so long
I look in your eyes, there's a distant light
And you and I know there'll be a storm tonight
This is getting serious
Are you thinking 'bout you or us?

Don't say what you're about to say
Look back before you leave my life
Be sure before you close that door
Before you roll those dice
Baby think twice

Baby think twice for the sake of our love, for the memory
For the fire and the faith that was you and me
Baby I know it ain't easy
When your soul cries out for higher ground
'Cause when you're halfway up, you're always halfway down
But baby this is serious
Are you thinking 'bout you or us?

Don't say what you're about to say
Look back before you leave my life
Be sure before you close that door
Before you roll those dice
Baby think twice

Baby this is serious
Are you thinking 'bout you or us?

CHAPTER 2

A Good Breakup Is Everything

Respect and Kindness

A love affair, or a marriage, is a journey. It is a grand number of decisions and compromises made by both sides, and it represents many steps taken. Sometimes, sadly, breaking up is another step in that journey. But how you do it will affect all that follows. If you intend to have a good divorce, a good break up is the smartest way to start it.

Breaking up is not a single conversation or simply one bad night. It is a series of reveals. It is the crossing of several thresholds. It is finally the realization that what was once great may now be done. You may come to this awakening in sync with your spouse, or a few steps ahead or a few steps behind. But how, when, and where you deliver the news or how you take the news, if it's you on the receiving end, is everything. The quality of the rest of your life is at stake. Break up respectfully, without embarrassing your spouse, and you may find that you have the opportunity to end your marriage without ruining everything that follows. Respect is the only way to make sure it unfolds the right way. Respect the fears, the sadness, the anger, and the worry. Maybe you are mad, but so is your spouse.

The person you are divorcing is not your mortal enemy, nor is he or she someone you suddenly have to despise. This is more than likely someone you have spent many years of your life with. You have made promises, made plans, maybe made children, and now made a mess of things. Just because you are about to divorce does not change the fact that once upon a time, you were completely in love and thought you two could conquer the future together and make each other's lives even better.

Okay, so that didn't happen. Things have not turned out like everyone planned. Sorry. Life is what happens. Not what you *hoped* would happen. You have to find comfort in the future more than you are consumed with regret for the past. You also have to help everyone else survive. Sadness is everywhere, as you would expect. The one thing you can provide to ameliorate it is kindness. The kindest version of yourself is the least you can give. Be kind to everyone, including your spouse, your children, your in-laws, everyone touched by the breaking up of the dream. Be willing to understand. Be open to hearing everything anyone wants to tell you. This will make the process you are about to go through that much easier for everyone else and yourself. And if my theory on all this is right—which it is—you will also be on the way to a good divorce.

No Messy Endings

If you leave your spouse with a heart full of deceptions and ears full of half-truths, he or she may never want to have anything to do with you again. Leave the right way. Take your time with this huge decision and its aftermath. Disaster awaits those who act like idiots and step confidently into an uncertain future, leaving one relationship upended and unended while beginning another with just as many doubts. If you want to have a good divorce, it cannot begin with you emerging from behind a curtain of lies to drop the big news that you're out of here. Messy endings and good divorces do not go together. The messy ending does not bring out the best in you nor your soon-to-be ex nor your soon-to-be next. And so easy to avoid.

Avoid a messy ending by planning for the end of the marriage. Yes, I said planning. This could be done in some proportion to the time you spent planning the wedding. If it took six months to get the wedding right, take three months to get the divorce right. Scuba divers say, "Plan the dive, dive the plan," as a way of keeping on track regardless of what happens under the water. Same idea here. Plan the divorce, and then divorce according to plan. Especially those first important and vital steps. This will allow you time to leave the relationship with a little dignity instead of rushing off stupidly because you misunderstood something someone said, or you let your jealous heart rule the day. Avoid the messy ending, and you just might not find all your most private and personal secrets divulged to the world via the internet because you pissed off your spouse with your childish behavior. No good reason to have a rushed and hurried farewell. Most human beings hate *bad* surprises.

Avoid a messy ending by letting a respectable amount of time pass before you jump into your next relationship. Maybe a month for every year you were together? Or if you're in that much of a hurry to waltz back into it, how about waiting at least until the next calendar year? Some amount of time that a reasonable person would consider respectful.

Avoid a messy ending by slamming nothing. No slammed doors or slammed phones. No slammed hands on kitchen counters or on the roofs of cars. No slamming anything, okay? That just makes endings very, very messy.

Avoid a messy ending by refusing to be a jerk. Even though it's headed in the direction of a divorce—and I use the term *headed* because until you are divorced, you're still married, and he or she still deserves your complete respect. Need I remind you that you loved this person so much, once upon a time, that you put them above all others and promised heart and soul forever? Just because forever came a lot earlier than you expected is no reason to forget all that was there in the beginning.

The Right Location

Where you and your spouse are when the conversation about the breakup begins in earnest is not as important as how and why, but it's important nonetheless. You do not want to begin the end of your relationship in a way that is hurtful or harmful or embarrassing or unkind.

When a very well-known film director broke up with one of his girlfriends, he had her over to his mansion for a nice dinner and then offered her a daylong shopping spree on Rodeo Drive in Beverly Hills. Though jilted, she never said a bad word about him and walked off with $150,000 worth of dresses and shoes and jewelry. Okay, so not everyone can throw down that much coin just to ease the pain, but the fact is that he handled it right, for him. It was private, it was gentle, it was respectful. And many years later, she remains one of his champions.

Most people would prefer to know that things aren't going well in a relationship the instant the other person feels that way. Deception of any kind is a felony, especially where love and relationships are concerned. So if you have something to say, just get on with it. Share the news, even if it's bad.

The journey to goodbye starts with a conversation, and *where* that conversation takes place tempers the first few steps and, ultimately, the tone and tenor of the entire breakup. There is no good place to have a conversation about breaking up a relationship or a marriage. There are only a few acceptable options and many more unacceptable ones. Unacceptable places include in your bed, in a restaurant, at somebody else's house, in the bathroom, on a long road trip, at a movie theater, in a cab, at your mother's house, at a ball game, or in a bar. Every one of these locales brings the focus of strangers or bartenders and waitresses or family members to one or both of you in an unforgettable and unforgivable way. And all will embarrass your soon-to-be ex. This is all the more true if your announcement is a complete surprise, and your soon to be ex start throwing things or throwing up, whichever comes first. This will make the breakup memorable for all the wrong reasons. And it will linger throughout the process and color the divorce (Imagine: "And you know where I found out it was over? At Marvin's Bar Mitzvah! Can you believe that?").

So where does one start a conversation to end a relationship? On the phone? Cowardly. In the middle of lunch in a crowded restaurant? Mean. At the tail end of an argument? Makes it appear that you were lying in wait (which you are, but why make it look that way?). Via text? Only if you're still in seventh grade. On Facebook? Equally juvenile. So that does not leave a lot of options.

The conversation you have to have will go on for days or weeks or months anyway. This is just the first step in a journey of a thousand miles or so. Here are some locations that will cause the least harm and embarrassment: At the breakfast table when it is just the two of you. In the car when it is just the two of you. In a park, where it is just the two of you. On a walk with the dog when it is just the two of you. You see the trend here, right? When you are delivering the terrible news to somebody, let it just be the two of you, wherever it is.

Then start the conversation with words like, "You're not going to like what I have to say." Or, "This is not going to be a great conversation." Or something equally kind that gives your spouse a few seconds to gather their defenses and be ready for whatever is next. And then immediately get to the point. Speak from the heart, and tell all the truth.

Avoid Starting Fights or Fires

My first wife and I were in the beginning of our breakup. There was still a chance we could get back together, but the chance was diminishing more every day, like a candle in a room with less and less oxygen. Every conversation would end with some uncomfortable bickering. It really didn't matter what the subject was, but it was increasingly difficult to keep the good-divorce train on the track when all these little fights would break out. I began to recognize that there were triggers to these skirmishes and that I needed to figure out what they were and avoid them. As anyone who has ever been in a troubled relationship knows, there are certain words or sounds or looks or motions that are intended for one, and only one, purpose, and that is to start an argument. They are like little Molotov cocktails that get thrown in the middle of the dry splintering wood of a dying love affair. Next thing you know, there is a huge booming sound, and the conversation is on fire. This is all the more the case when a divorce is hanging in the balance. Both you and the soon-to-be ex are feeling extremely sensitive, prone to an outburst, out of patience with each other, and quicker to anger than either of you should be.

So I asked several people smarter than me, including two psychologists, about the concept of words, sounds, or motions that deliberately antagonize the other person and set a conversation on fire. They pointedly agreed that these kinds of triggers absolutely exist, especially with a divorcing couple.

Here are some examples:

a) The word *always*—As in, "You *always* do that when I'm finally feeling happy." Or, "Just like you *always* do, you're trying to ruin this for me too."

b) The word *never*—As in, "You *never* let me finish saying how I feel." Or, "Why is it that you *never* come home on time?"

c) The unintelligible mutter—This is some people's best trick. It is something kinda awful spoken just softly enough so that the person you are saying it to cannot quite hear it but still gets terribly offended. The most common response you'll hear is, "What did you just say?"

d) A look of complete doubt—You know the look. It is a facial expression meant to imply that whatever the other person is saying is completely unbelievable. Its purpose is simply to start something, something bad. Looks of complete doubt include rolling the eyes, slowly shaking the head from side to side, pursing the lips, dropping the "fade," offering the fish eye, a blank stare, a wince, or the ever-popular grimace.

e) The insulting sound effect—Conversational sound effects have one intention and one intention only: to diminish or otherwise show scorn for the person those noises are directed toward. Sound effects that turn a normal conversation into a bonfire include the long sigh, the deprecating *tsk-tsk*, the low whistle, the outright groan, the fake sneeze (that sounds a lot like the word *bull*—), the completely phony cough, or the pretend rim shot. All of these start fires.

f) The soundless insult, aka the mime—Most often, these silent bomblets are delivered courtesy of your hands and include several nonverbal slights, such as throwing hands in the air, holding your head in your hands, clamping your hand over your mouth, or waving *go away*. There's also the always popular extended middle finger, the too-much-talk/blah-blah-blah motion, or the Vegas blackjack dealer's spread hands farewell. Any one or all of these will send the conversation with you and your soon to-be-ex right over the edge, into the fiery pits of hell.

Starting fires will not help you have a nice breakup or a good divorce. If you can, stop doing it. But if you like to watch a barn burn, then go on ahead. Do it at your own peril. Deliberately starting fights or fires is one of the many ways you can ruin your chances for an otherwise good divorce.

Hear the Other Person's News First

There is a commercial for the California Lottery that ran a few years ago in which a man and his girlfriend are sitting in a car during a rainstorm, and they both have exciting news for each other. She says to the man, "You go first," knowing that her news is better than his news no matter what.

He says okay, takes a deep breath, looks over at her, and says, "I want to break up."

She looks back at him and says, "I just won the lottery!"

Great messaging. Great commercial too. And the point is clearly to try and never let this kind of thing happen to you. Even if you are in the right place, armed with the right line, and finally ready to begin the break up, still ask a lot of questions and find out everything you can before you commence to commence. Always hear the other person's news first. Suppose he or she just inherited a few million. Or wants to break up with you. Anything's possible.

Tell the Truth

Vital to a good divorce is a good breakup and a kind goodbye. This requires you to be forthright, to speak all your truth, to not embarrass your spouse. Announce your sad intentions with the greatest amount of dignity you can pull together. Anything less and you will be remembered for the lousy goodbye and not much else. Say you're leaving the same day you announce the bankruptcy, then you're twice a jerk. It will be a really long and nasty goodbye. That will be the thing that defines you, no matter how nice you are later.

It does not have to be this way and never did. Most people would prefer a direct and straightforward missive. They want all the news that's fit to print. They want to know that you don't love them anymore *the minute* that you don't love them anymore. Not a year or five years or ten years later. They want to know everything there is to know that instant.

Save everyone a great deal of time and trouble. Be straightforward and truthful, and you will start the break up the right way. The impact will last forever.

The Worst Breakup Ever

One of my uncles died when I was young, though he remained a figure in my life for many years after. I revered him but never knew him. We never had coffee or shared manly stories or any of that kind of thing. He never met either of my wives or my children, but nonetheless, he was a force in my life. I was always seeking out a conversation with people who knew him, thinking that if I could collect enough bits and pieces, I might be able to make some sort of collage of who he was and what he might have been to me. Admittedly this is like trying to fill a sieve with water, but I kept on searching, nonetheless. I would look up his former wives, business associates, secretaries, actors, friends, biographers, anyone.

This all came to a beautiful conclusion when I found myself on the phone with a woman who was his closest confidante for more than a decade, also his mistress and girlfriend, and if that wasn't enough, his secretary and script girl. Her name, for the purposes of this story, was M, and they inhabited an office together at one of the big studios in Hollywood. That he was married to someone else or attracted to other women for several of the years they were together did not seem to diminish her feelings for him or that they had for each other. It was one of those legendary Hollywood love affairs, at least according to most of the biographers.

I felt very comfortable asking her to be completely honest with me and tell me exactly what kind of man my uncle really was. After all, if anyone would know, it would have been her. "For real?" she asked me.

I said yes. I was expecting a tribute. Instead I got a torpedo. She said, "You really want to know…about him and what kind of a person he really was? Well, I'll tell you something…he was a liar and an asshole."

"What? What did you say?" I gasped. It caught me so off guard I burst out laughing.

"You heard me," she said. "He was a liar and an asshole."

It took me a minute to catch my balance. But I finally did. The only things people had ever said to me about him were so overwhelmingly complimentary that I was not used to hearing him referred to as anything less than a god. But there it was. The woman who knew him better than anyone else in the world thought he was a thoughtless imbecile. I prodded her to tell me what happened that would cause her to say that about him. I told her that it sounded to me like she was carrying around the residual memory of one awful thing rather than the collective memory of their many years together.

"So what did he do?" I asked.

She told me the story of young M. Actress, beauty queen, pinup girl, dancer, all-around cutie pie. She had come to Hollywood in the 1950s to earn her living in the bright lights and on the silver screen. She hooked up with my uncle early on but never gave up the dream of being a successful actress. Finally, one day came along, and she got her chance at last. My uncle cast her as "the girl" in a movie he was directing. M was finally going to get out from behind the camera and get herself in front of it. She was so excited she told everyone who would listen, and everyone listened. It was going to be one of the great moments of her life.

Then about a week before principal photography was to begin, she was invited up to the lead actor's house. For tea. Not Hollywood tea, real tea. She didn't know what to expect. But brave and full of pluck and muster, she rang the big doorbell. Whatever she was expecting, she did not expect the bomb that he dropped on her. The star of the film told her that a decision had been made, and she was off the picture, no longer the lead actress, and that he and my uncle had found someone else for the role. Someone a little younger, a little better suited for the part. She sat there, not knowing what to say. Her hands shaking and her mouth dry and her cheeks suddenly flushed red with embarrassment. He then said, "And there's something else."

What could this be? she thought. Everything she had dreamed about was already gone.

He said, "And our director has fallen in love with this other actress as well." Talk about your bad goodbyes. My uncle had done the unthinkable. *He sent in a friend to do the breaking up for him!* He did this to a woman he had been with for years. It was unbelievable. I always wanted to hope my uncle was the greatest guy ever, but then to learn that he had performed an incredibly cowardly and unscrupulous act and to learn it from the woman he did it to left me stupefied. And a little ashamed. And embarrassed. He had someone break up *for* him? He *really* did that?

I thought very poorly of my dear uncle at that moment and said as much to his former girlfriend, then an eighty-three-year-old woman who remembered the insult of that awful goodbye like he had slapped her across the face only yesterday. Many years had passed, but her cheek still stung. After a moment or two of making sense of what I had just heard, I told M that I realized there was no way to ever make up for all the hurt. What he had done was unconscionable. I apologized from the bottom of my heart. And never forgot it either.

How you say goodbye is how you will be remembered.

If you leave a pregnant wife for your intern, she will correctly remember you as a complete ass. Everything that happens after that will be a grind between you. If you leave an ailing husband for his best friend, you'll look like a liar and a thief. How you say goodbye is one of the most vital and important parts of the journey of your relationship. Slam a door, and that is what your ex will tell everyone. Throw a tantrum and storm out the night before your sister's wedding, and that's who you are. That's how you are going to be remembered. You will always be the callous selfish lump you proved yourself to be at the moment of the breakup.

For M, my uncle's terrible goodbye was "a bar across her heart." It was an act of romantic savagery. It prevented her from loving and dreaming and living life to its fullest. My uncle took away much more than a part in a movie. He literally took away her reason for happiness. It was, by any measure, an act that was completely unforgivable.

When it is time to break up with someone, particularly the person you have been sharing your life with for however many years, be honest. Be truthful. Be direct. Yes, it will be embarrassing and awkward and awful in its own way because sad truths are always hard to deliver. But the sadder the truth, the better it is delivered in person, by one person to the other, with just the two of you there. Respectfully. Kindly. Truthfully. Face to face.

And There's Always the New Year's Eve Option

As unsure as my mom may have been about some things she did in her life, one thing she was never in doubt about was when to break up with someone. Whether that someone was one of her three husbands, a boyfriend, or even just a friend, she would not go into a new year with them unless she was absolutely sure she wanted them around for *the whole year*. She would say, "Not another *year* with that so-and-so…"

This policy saved her the agony of making quick emotionally charged decisions. Instead of waiting for the final piece of evidence that a particular relationship was going nowhere, she had a date certain to confirm it. She always knew that New Year's Eve was coming, and if she was not still impressed by Ralph, Bill, or Jimmy, Chuck, Pat, or Barry, there was a great opportunity to lop off their heads, metaphorically speaking, as the new year was to begin. The New Year's Eve breakup was always at the ready for her. She preferred to look at her romances and friendships like they were on a one-year lease, like a new Buick. Whoever she was with had a year with her, her heart, her company, her companionship, etc. But it was always at her option as to whether or not to extend it.

So as you work yourself into the position of deciding whether or not to end things and move on, consider the new year as a hurdle over which the relationship must jump if it is to survive. Do you want to spend a whole entire year with the person you are somewhat unsure of? Do you want to let something that is not working very well drag on past another Valentine's Day, St. Patrick's Day, Labor Day? You get the point, right? If you're not happy, and you know you're not going to be happy anytime soon, maybe you don't go into another year.

Should you decide on this course of action, please say it respectfully, kindly, gently, lovingly. Say it like you would want to hear it.

CHAPTER 3

Having a Good Divorce

Let the Lawyer Do the Heavy Lifting

The last thing you want to do is handle *any* aspect of the divorce yourself. It will be messy. It will blow up in your face. It will do damage that will last for years, if not forever. Hire a lawyer you trust, and then trust them to look after your interests. That way, when something goes wrong—which it will—or someone's feelings get hurt—which they will—or an outrageous request is floated—which it will—you have complete deniability. And by the way, once the lawyers are involved, everything gets turned up like crazy anyway. Their job is to bring the heat and bring it strong and make the other side worried and weak. "Practically scary," is how one friend of mine described it. Like the Geico commercial says, that's just what they do. But if you can put a little distance between you and your lawyer, you can protect yourself and maintain the possibility of a good divorce.

Your lawyer is your mouthpiece. Let them do all the work and all the talking and all the negotiating and all the delivering of good and bad news. The whole process will go much smoother if you have little to do with it. You can spend your time caretaking your family through the very difficult waters in which they are trying to stay afloat. When in doubt, blame the lawyer. Maintain your relationship with your spouse and move things forward to the ultimate resolution and the possibility of a less-hostile situation afterward.

"My lawyer said that?" you can say to your ex. "Don't worry, I'll talk to that a-hole and make it right."

If you let your lawyer do and say all the difficult things that have to be done and said in a divorce, you can ensure that your soon-to-be ex will not lose their mind over some needless details, and you can continue to play the part of good spouse, something the family probably got accustomed to after all those years with you.

In most states, there are clear rules for divorce and dissolution of community property, and the courts have already set the standard for what each side can expect from the other. You plug in your assets, the number of years you were together, the number of children, and then an app tells you what your obligations are going to be for the next few years or for the rest of your life. And there's no negotiation because that is the law, as decided by decades of judges and appellate courts and supreme courts and all the appeals and so on. It is what it is.

When my first wife and I finally got around to having a lawyer involved, months into the process of us divorcing, I asked a man who I knew very well to be the lawyer, *and he agreed to be the lawyer for both sides.* He was more like a mediator. He would call her, and then he would call me. And then her, and then me. She wanted this, I wanted that. She requested this, and in exchange, I got to request that. And so on it went. He guided us to a place where both of us were fine with the final result. He would tell us if something was too much (and in one case, too little) and advise what a judge might say about it. Things proceeded like this until every detail was almost resolved, and we were down to a few very minor issues. The very final discussion actually took place at a bar over a martini and a couple of glasses of wine. It was all very pleasant and led us to the place we find ourselves now— very friendly, without resentment or any lingering animosity.

We kept our eye on the ball, knowing that the divorce was just another step in the journey of our relationship, *not the last step in that journey!* We are parents, both involved and invested in our two children. We are the son and daughter of our mutually shared parents. We are champions of each other's lives and careers. All this is easy to do because there were no terrible things to forget that should never have been said in the first place. She got most of what she wanted, and so did I. It all went down like this because we let the lawyer do the heavy lifting.

Generosity Is an Investment in Your Future

The more generous you are, the more gracious and graceful your divorce will be. The more generous you are, the greater the dividends and royalties it will bring to your existence later. The more generous you are, the more benefits it will bring you and all your future relationships. As a for instance, with a good divorce, you will not be sued several more times by your ex for additional funding (more on this later) because he or she will have gotten plenty in the first place and won't need any of your new money. As another for instance, with a good divorce, your ex will not tell your children you were unkind and ungenerous. There will be little reason to say such terrible things, as there will be no evidence for it. The more generous you are, the greater the likelihood that you can have a decent and workable and loving relationship with your ex and your children going forward. Because they will be living a good life, hopefully, thanks to your thoughtfulness. As a final for instance, your generosity means that you do not have to make all your friends decide which of you two they are going to be friends with in the future. Because they can continue to be friends with both of you. Because they can invite both of you to their homes, their barbecues, their graduations, and so on. Be generous, and there will be no "enemy" in the divorce, just two people moving on with their lives.

Your generosity will also buy you peace. Peace of mind, peace of heart, peace of place, peace of future. You have a debt to your ex, and you paid it, end of story. If you choose to write a check every month, it will be like another mortgage, and when you finally write the last check, it will be a feeling of satisfaction and accomplishment like no other. If you write just one check, as I wholeheartedly recommend that you do, you will be financially free from that day forward.

In the state of California, the divorce capitol of the United States, there are so many divorces that they have devised a computer program to make it easier on everyone and cut down on the long lines at the courthouses throughout the state. They even have a cute name for it, the Dissomaster. But that's California. Maybe they have something else in New York and something else in Florida, I wouldn't know. But however the courts near you fast track the divorce process, figure out what it recommends you pay over the next many years, and let that be the *minimum* you provide. If you can pay more, pay more. Pay more and do it now while there is still some money to do that with. My friend Mike, one of the richest and smartest guys I know, gave me this advice. When he got divorced from his wife, he figured out what the Dissomaster would recommend and then doubled it. Mind you, he was a wealthy guy who had plenty to give, but he didn't waste a penny or a minute trying to get the price down. He found a nice round number and wrote a big check. I see his ex all the time, mainly because they have stayed such close friends. He helps her manage her life and her investments, and he even helps her manage the properties she bought with her divorce monies. She thinks the world of him. And why wouldn't she? He handled the business of his divorce with incredible generosity.

Why shouldn't your divorce be the same way? Why shouldn't your ex continue to love and respect you, long after you're not sleeping together anymore? Why not have your ex actually cheer for you later on, in your business and career and personal decisions? Suppose you have more children with a new spouse. Wouldn't it be good to have everyone's kids get along with everyone else's? The generosity guideline applies whether you have millions or thousands or hundreds that you are dividing between you.

Many years ago, I worked alongside a finance company that was intimately involved in the lives of many successful professional athletes. One of these superstars had gotten a girl pregnant. For whatever reasons, he had no intention of marrying her. He was looking for a quick out. The solution he came up with, all on his own, was to put a down payment on a condo and walk. She would have to make all the payments going forward. Needless to say, neither she nor her many lawyers were going to go along with that, and they were prepared to sue him for all his cake. The head of the finance company called another superstar athlete client more experienced in such matters. He put both superstars on the phone. Imagine Tom Brady and Tiger Woods—although it's not either of them. The veteran told the rookie that the only way out of any of the lawsuits was to be exceedingly generous.

It was good advice, and as a result, the rookie's pregnant girlfriend never went to court, and nothing was ever said in the press about any of it. Because of his generosity, whether heartfelt or as a career-salvaging move, his life went on without interruption. Yes, of course all the parties had to sign an eighty-page settlement, but the soon-to-be mother was okay to sign it because the athlete ultimately showed her complete respect and was very generous.

A former writer of mine, Curtis Jackson (a.k.a. 50 Cent), had a big hit with another Universal writer, Neyo, on this very subject. It was called "Baby by Me." I had shared the story of the overly thrifty athlete with him and his team as a cautionary tale, a warning of what could happen to them. Maybe that advice inspired him to write the song, but who knows for sure. I would like to think so! (See Appendix 2 for a list of some of the other writers I signed.)

It's unlikely that most people reading along here can afford to buy their exes houses or would even want to. But that's not the point. 50 Cent's story illustrates the overriding value of generosity when ending relationships. It sets the tone for all that follows, especially if the ultimate goal is to have a good divorce.

Write One Check and Pay Everything All at Once

I play golf with a man who divorced his wife fifteen years ago and still writes her a check every month. He approaches this moment like it's a prostate exam with a witch doctor. He anticipates how bad it will be and is rarely disappointed. The monthly check is an obligation he has to his wife that she is not even thankful for anymore. His monthly sacrifice is her routine expectation. His misery absolutely influenced my divorce. I realized that I did not want that same type of grinding animus to stretch into my future. I was making a lot of money at the time, so I knew I had some big financial obligations to attend to, but I also needed to know that there would be an end to them someday.

So taking both a cue and some advice from my friend Mike, mentioned earlier, I figured out how to pay off everything in one big check as opposed to hundreds of smaller ones. I paid one big lump sum, which included everything and anything that I might owe my ex and to support my children. In so doing, I got the divorce over with and all my financial responsibilities settled on the same day! It was the day we signed the papers. She was happy. I was happy. That was the end of the check-writing, once and for all. Here's what I did.

Since we had been married for over ten years, California law granted her an incredible array of rights and moneys and payments, which would have stretched well into my dotage or thereabouts. And among the package of rights was the right to expect a check from me every month for that entire period of time. So instead I added up all the obligations that I would have had and put them on one side of the ledger. Inclusive of alimony, child support, colleges, vacations, some extras, and inflation, the total was nearly $1 million, to be paid out over the next many years or until I died. What a comforting thought, I thought.

We then put all our assets, including the house and the savings and life insurance and so forth, and put them on the other side of that same ledger. We divided the assets in half, and then from my half of the assets, we deducted the obligations, the $1 million or whatever it was. Thanks to some good real estate moves and my Irish resistance to pissing away cash when it was plentiful, half my share of the assets was actually *greater* than my total financial obligations to my wife and kids. I quitclaimed the house and its mortgage and debt to her, and the amount left over was what *she owed me*. I lost the house but got financial independence in return. As a result of this arrangement, I have never written even one additional check and had zero obligations going forward. Free and clear. One and done. Over and out.

The arrangement was as good for her and the family as it was for me. She got to keep the house she loved, and my boys got to stay in the house they were born into and grew up in. I had the chance to start all over again without any weights around my ankles. There were no lifelong financial obligations holding me back from whatever was yet to come. I followed my kind heart and generous instinct and saved myself the monthly ritual that has diminished the lives of several pals.

I am aware that not everyone can afford this kind of move. It's expensive. But I include the story to encourage you to think creatively about these kinds of elements in your divorce. Talk to your spouse. There may be things he or she wants more than you. These might be easy for you to give up in exchange for some things you may want more. In my case, I wanted complete financial freedom, and she wanted the house. We cut a deal that worked for both of us and never looked back. There was no need. Everyone was satisfied with the arrangement.

A Solution to the Custody Fight

The custody of the children is the land mine in most divorces. It is one of the most contentious issues to be faced, and it is often a major turning point in the divorce proceedings. By turning point, I mean where it turns from bad to really bad. Even if the divorce had been a somewhat-reasonable process up until then. Once custody is on the table, things will likely go straight to hell. Why, you ask? Several reasons. It's the lawyer's last chance to make up for any previous losses in the negotiations. It's the last chance to see the the other side squirm. It is the final moment of the drama that was a marriage and is now a tragic opera. It is the last chance for one side to punish the other by denying the happiness that would be time with the kids. Custody is also the easiest way an angry or resentful spouse can try to build a bigger wall between the children and the other parent.

I knew a couple whose friendship did not survive the divorce. He was not generous; she was not kind. It went down to the wire, getting more bitter with every exchange between the lawyers, who were under orders from their clients to play hardball at every opportunity. And so they did. The battle became especially heated when it came to the custody of the children. Since this was the last issue to be decided, the lawyers were like Rocky and Apollo Creed, or as they called it, another day at the office. An enmity was created between the couple that will never dissipate. In the end, the mother got the majority of the time with the children, and the father's time was very specifically detailed and included time penalties if he was to bring them home late, even from trips or soccer games or other situations that he was not in control of. This was the penalty he had to pay for being an a-hole during the divorce, and he pays for it still. She was not required to tell him what the kids were doing or where they were going or what their lives were like without him, so as a result, he was left totally outside their circle.

I do not know what exactly the lawyers were thinking when they decided the war between this family was going to come down to the custody of the children. Maybe they were just extending their billable hours, or maybe they were trying to show each other who was who in case they ever faced each other again in another divorce. Whatever the reasoning, both sides lost. But the real loser was the dad. The children felt relaxed at their mother's home and on edge at their father's. There were no clocks at the mom's house, and they were always *on the clock* at their dad's. The father was always playing catch-up and pressing them for the details of their lives because he was getting none of these from their mother, and so the visits became more and more like interrogations. A disastrous time was being had by all. The kids got closer to the mom and further from the dad, and that's how things stand to this day. She won. He lost.

Here's a truth I learned and one that I came to realize fully during my divorce—home is more likely where the mother lives. You the man can pretend that your apartment is just as nice and just as friendly. But it ain't. And it never will be as special as the home your children grew up in. All your kids' memories of home and family and love and together- ness are wrapped up in their memories of the place in which all those things were experienced. Namely their house.

I was aware of the disaster that awaited me if I wanted a long drawn-out custody battle with my first wife over our two little guys, who, at the time of the divorce, were twelve and seven. So I chose another solution to the problem. All I really cared about was how much *time* I got with my sons. *Where* that time was spent was not as important. And I did not want a judge or a panel of experts to decide how much time was enough nor how much time was going to be too much. So my proposal to my soon-to-be ex was simple. I offered her 100 percent custody in exchange for 100 percent visitation rights. In other words, they could live with her for- ever and always, but I could see them any day and anytime I wanted, provided it didn't present a conflict with school or play or sports or family time with their mom. The result was that I saw my boys almost every day. As they were growing up, I was a constant in their lives, as if I still lived with them. I would pick them up and take them to school. I coached them in every single sport that was available. I drove them to birthday parties and practices and picked them up afterward. I was never *not* there, except when I was on business out of town. Having me around was the rule and not the exception. I saw them or talked to them both almost every day, and it would be a big surprise if I were to go more than two days without a visit, a hug and a kiss, a quick listen to a story of the day, or whatever it was they had available.

What my ex wanted more than anything else was a sense of home, and nothing would give her this feeling more than continuing to live with her boys. By giving her all that she wanted in this regard—namely her boys always living with her—I got what I wanted: unlimited time with them to do whatever there was to do, whenever I wanted to do it. According to her, I may have spent more time with them after we got divorced. Those two boys are now twenty-eight and twenty-two, and very thankful to me for how I handled the divorce overall. But they are very, *very* thankful for the way I handled the issue of their custody. They got to stay in the house they grew up in, in their own rooms, and the divorce of their parents did not destroy their sense of home and family.

By giving my ex 100 percent custody in exchange for 100 percent visitation, I was able to sidestep one of the most dangerous and explosive issues that face a divorcing couple. I made sure to rent and then subsequently own a new place just a few blocks away too. I saw my boys all the time, at least every day, and she enjoyed the greater privilege of living with them. She probably came out a little better in the deal than I did, admittedly, but if that was one of the payments for my good divorce, it was time and money and rights well spent. But I also got much more time with them in the long run than I would have gotten with a big custody battle. Lots of time with my boys made a grand and great difference in my life, regardless of whose house they lived in.

Not sure this gambit will work for everyone, but I include it to suggest that you are not locked into anything. Figure out what you want and exchange it with your soon-to-be ex for something else. For me it was all the time in the world with my boys. For her, it was them living in her house. We both got what we wanted. We both won.

When in Doubt About What to Say, Say Nothing

It is hard to put into words how important it is to just keep your mouth shut during the process of your divorce. Take my word for it, and the word of the thousands and millions of people who have trodden this same road before you, it is *that* important. If you can just keep quiet and say nothing, things will go more smoothly for you, in the short term and the long run. Any attempt to get in one last zinger before you end a conversation is time wasted. And energy lost. Just say nothing. Say nothing about anything. Just don't. For the sake of you and your better future, just leave it alone. Unkind things must go unsaid. *Must go unsaid.* No need to destroy a beautiful past just because there's no future.

People, it turns out, never forget anything, especially if it's a bad thing. Any remarks that hint, however broadly, disparaging youth or weight or beauty or anything else, just cannot be spoken. *There is no place for unkind statements in a good divorce.* Imagine that anything awful you say might as well be tattooed on your face. It will be there, and it will never go away. Like Mike Tyson and that symbol. Forever.

There is an old Sicilian proverb that my ex-father-in-law often used. It had to do with the importance of keeping one's mouth shut at all times. And it was wisdom that I lived by throughout my divorce with his daughter. In Italian, it's like this, "*Una pesca morta quando boca aperto.*" It translates into this, "A fish dies with its mouth open." In other words, if you keep your thoughts to yourself, you will live to see another day. I did not want to be that dead fish, and I never was. I just kept my piehole closed up tight and kept on swimming. And if you want to get through your divorce with your mind and soul intact, don't be that fish either. Just keep the negative comments to yourself. This guidance applies to all your conversations with, for, about, or to your soon-to-be ex. Say nothing to anyone other than that you wish him or her well. Not a negative word to anyone. Just say nothing and have yourself a good divorce.

Guilt Has No Value in a Good Divorce

There's a big difference between being generous and being ridiculous. One of the principal forces that can cause a divorce to slip from one action to the other is a feeling of guilt about the marriage not working out. Regret, remorse, whatever you want to call it, it's all the same thing. You both made all those promises you will be unable to keep. Now you're giving him or her back to the world and, on some level, feeling very bad about it. Guilt is the motivator because deep inside, you wish you could have done better. No matter how hard your tried, maybe you could have tried harder. No matter how much you compromised, maybe you could have compromised more. No matter how much you gave, maybe you could have given even more. And maybe you always meant to do that someday too. But regardless of how badly you may feel, guilt cannot become part of the transaction of your divorce.

Okay, so you feel terrible about how everything collapsed. We all understand and sympathize with you. But it stops there. Your guilt has no financial value in this process, and I implore you to not spend a penny because of it. Guilt dollars are the dumbest dollars you will ever throw away. Why? Because you will be getting nothing in return. And you won't feel that much better about it anyway. Okay, so you feel bad. You cannot make that feeling go away with this kind of outlay. The marriage is over, and that's really all that matters. Guilt money is something you must stay away from. It is a momentary feeling of false relief. But at the same time, it is something you will probably consider forking over. And your ex, most likely encouraged by lawyers, will push you hard for it as well. But don't fall for it. Pay your alimony, pay your child support, be generous as hell, but do not—repeat—do not put up a penny for guilt.

One friend of mine fell in love with someone new and was divorcing an otherwise very nice wife, which happened to be his second one at that point. He felt terrible about how things turned out. He was almost consumed by his guilt. And she egged him on at every turn. She told him it was all his fault. She told him she felt betrayed. She just kept squeezing his nuts on this point (and not in a good way) and made it clear she felt the demise of the marriage was 100 percent his doing. Which it was, but so what? There was only a fifty-fifty chance in the first place. But feeling the heat, he not only paid off her mortgage, he let her walk away with all the rights and royalties to a TV show she had created *during their marriage* that would ultimately become a hit and give her several big paydays.

What did he get for his sacrifice? He got squat. What did she get for manipulating him like that? Millions. Why did he let all this go? Guilt, nothing more. Why did he turn his back on all that money? Because he felt so bad that it didn't all work out. He felt it was all his fault. And it was, but like I said earlier, so what?

She kept telling him that she thought they were going to be together forever, blah-blah-blah. Hey, I used to believe in the Easter Bunny. My friend's soon-to-be ex ground her high heel into the top of his bare foot. She hammered him on this point and made it like the only way she would ever feel better again is if he gave up his rights to her show. Which he did. And cost himself a fortune.

Don't let this happen to you! Things happen. Life happens. If you are going to be a nice person, make sure you get rewarded for it, respected for it, remembered for it. And if that's not going to happen, then don't feel guilty about what's going down. Pay what you owe and be as generous as you can possibly be. But nothing more. Especially not for guilt.

The Emotions Will Keep on Coming

During the process of your divorce, whether it's a six-month quickie or a three-year war, the emotions will be overwhelming sometimes. How could they not be? You are going through one of the most difficult and tumultuous times you will ever know. Be prepared for these emotions to show up anytime and anywhere. Especially when they are least expected. Should any of these find purchase in your heart, reach out to a friend or therapist to talk them out. In time, their impact will diminish. I kept track of the ones that shadowed me most and list them here.

1. *Anger* that this happened to me too
2. *Helplessness*, being beholden to a system that could care less
3. *Panic*, knowing my future was no longer in my control
4. *Heartbreak*, knowing my marriage was really and truly over
5. *Sadness* being suddenly so distant from my soon to be ex and my boys.
6. *Regret* that it finally came to this
7. *Emptiness*, no longer being head of my household
8. *Fear* of having to start all over again

One or all of these will find you too. Be aware and wary of their place in your life and do all you can to limit their impact on your heart and mind.

A Good Divorce Has to Be Good for Both Sides

I ran into the son of one of the world's best drummers. We started talking about divorce and how it impacts children. His normal mom and famous dad had gotten through their divorce when he was much younger, but it still didn't sit well with him. He then made a summary observation that was very clearly a reflection of his own situation and that of his parents. He said, "If it's not good for both sides, it will not be a good divorce."

Apparently the father, the drummer, had a much better attorney than the wife did, and this guy danced circles around the wife's attorney. The wife could not afford a top-flight lawyer, and she got what she paid for. So much so that the split of property and assets was completely unbalanced, leaving the dad with much more stuff, leaving the wife a minimal amount of cash to scrape by on. Meanwhile she was raising the two kids and living with them in her new apartment, which was less friendly and unbelievably less safe. Drummer dad got to keep the house. The kids mainly wanted to be at their dad's, which the court had determined should only happen three days a week and every other weekend. The mom was left in a no-win situation, and it wore on her badly. Her kids were always ready to go to the dad's house rather than her apartment. She got unhappy and stayed that way. Not so for the dad. According to his son, the dad knew that he had really gotten away with it, gotten away with something pretty rare. He had outsmarted his wife, outlawyered her lawyer, kept his house, and created the beginning of an unresolvable tension between her and her children. He won, and he won big, and he knew it. The son said he could imagine his father and the father's lawyer giving each other high fives on the way out of the courthouse, knowing that they got her and good. The son looked at me and said, "It was so unfair to my mom. She didn't do anything wrong, but my dad was just ready to move on."

His resentment about his dad's handling of the divorce rested as on him like rust. He knew it had been a bad divorce for his mom because the father bullied her right out of the nice life she was having. Not everyone can claim they won their divorce, but his father did and let everyone know it.

But did he really win? Okay, so he came out with more cash and more toys and got his wife out of the way so he could move on to whatever was next. But what about the residual impact of his divorce? What about what his children think and feel about his actions toward their mom? What about the bullying and meanness that the father is teaching his children is okay? What about all the dreams that died in the son's heart watching his mom move into her new apartment and descend into her new life? What about the fact that the son recognizes that his dad was a complete asshole to his mom? It's his mom, dude. Was it really worth it?

Bottom line, the father could have been a better man. He should have been. He could have given more and given her a much better situation without impacting his world at all. He was a rich guy with a great lawyer, and he came out on top. Woo-hoo. But the son rightfully resents his father, and the carryover is that he respects him much less than he would have if the father had simply been fair and kind and generous. If you don't mind that your children tell the world you are a conniving jerk, then go on ahead. Outfox the mother of your children and her attorney. Keep her alimony to the lowest possible level. Keep her child support, likewise, at the bare minimum. Make sure her happiness is just out of reach. Is that really how you want things to be?

For it to be a good divorce, it has to be good for both sides. If the mom gets the majority of the material assets, and the dad has to live like a pauper, then that is not fair and should not be allowed to happen, regardless of the rights available under the law. If the father drained the community coffers and kept all the money he was making in hidden accounts, then that is not fair and not right either, regardless of how happy it makes his lawyer and accountant to screw over the ex. It's not just about the money. It's about the afterward too. Whatever you do, your kids will know if it was fair or not. Your kids will know if you treated their mom or dad with respect and honor or not. If you lock your ex up in a lousy situation that can never be gotten out of, your kids will know what you did, and they likely will never forgive you, like the drummer's son never forgave his dad.

If you want a good divorce, then bring all the respect and generosity you can muster and present your best offer. The goal of a divorce cannot be simply about getting more than your ex. Instead, see it as a chance to show your kids and the world how fair you can be.

CHAPTER 4

Divorced, Moving Forward

First Things First

Once the divorce is over, and the papers are signed, and you have found a new place to live, then the next chapter in your life can begin. The upheaval that has been your world can begin to calm. New routines, new friends, and even new loves await, as all your new normals are established. There will be more time alone, more time to think about things that have happened, more peace probably than you've known in a while too. Congratulations. You have survived one of life's greatest challenges.

One of the new elements, and one of the most important, will be the new relationship you have with your ex. Now that you are not together as a couple, you and your ex will have to find a new way to relate to each other. This relationship will guide most of the interactions you have with your children, your in-laws, and all the mutual friends you used to share. *All of these people will see you as your ex sees you.* So if it's not working well with him or her, then it's not going to work well with any of them either. And of course, the vice versa is also true. If you two find a good balance and sure footing going into the next phase of your lives, then everyone else will go along.

When you see each other out in the world, how will you react? How do you introduce each other? Do you shake hands or hug? Do you give each other a little kiss on the cheek? When you are at a family gathering, like a dinner or a wedding, what happens? And suppose one of you is with your "next," what then? Because you have seen so much through each other's eyes, whatever you decide, it has to be in a manner that honors all the time and shared courage.

An ex-wife is not like an ex-girlfriend. She shared a life with you, not an apartment. An ex-husband is not yesterday's news. He's living breathing testimony to your beautiful past. You made promises to each other that you will not be keeping. And if you have children together, you have a mutual responsibility to help those little people establish the parameters of their own beautiful lives. You almost have no choice. You must make every effort to maintain a good relationship with your ex, teaching your children that the divorce was a step forward in both your lives, not a step off a high cliff for either one of you. If you don't have children, then things are that much simpler. You can part that much more easily because the future will be much simpler to deal with than the recent past has been.

Many people, according to all the data, would prefer some kind of a friendship with their exes rather than an estrangement that stifles and lingers. You can let this guide you because this next phase in the relationship will probably be the one that lasts you both for the rest of your lifetimes. Accepting it, whatever it is, will be key to your ongoing happiness. Obviously what was is gone and what's next is still in the process of being discovered. And what will become the relationship between the two of you is something altogether changed from that which you have known up until now.

The key to succeeding in this key moment in your life is to be open to everything that awaits, to approach the changes without preconditions and prejudice, and to accept your new role in all the lives you want to stay a part of.

Your relationship with your ex is not over by any means. It is simply changing. It is finding a new form. It will be different than it ever was before and might even be better and healthier than it has been in years. Read on, and you will see how I handled it.

Now for Something Completely Different

My relationship with my ex was always changing anyway. It was constantly evolving. And once we got divorced, it had to make even more changes, at least if the friendship we had developed and earned was going to survive in some form. Because of the divorce, our friendship was like the caterpillar turning itself into the butterfly. We were going from husband and wife into something very different, and neither of us had any idea what it would look like.

She wasn't my wife anymore, and I wasn't her husband anymore. We were forced to look at each other differently, to treat each other differently, to speak to each other differently. There were now a number of subjects that were no longer shareable and a number of questions that were no longer askable. I could offer counsel but not advice. I could gently chastise but never scold. I could be completely honest about everything because there was nothing between us to stop me from being so. If a dress made her look bad, *and she asked me about it*, I would tell her. If she had on too much makeup *and asked me about it*, I could tell her that too. If she made a mistake, *and she asked my opinion*, I would absolutely let her know my thoughts. As long as she asked me, there was nothing I could not discuss with her because I knew her better than anyone else on the planet. Come on. We had children together. I watched her give birth. I held her close when her heart broke. I dried her tears when she learned that a friend was actually not a friend at all. I had seen her in practically every situation.

She knew that I still wanted her to succeed. She knew I wanted her to be happy. She knew that I wanted her to be in love with her new guy and have it also be one of the greatest loves she had ever known, ala Brigitte Bardot. There was no point and no purpose in being jealous or possessive about the woman who used to be my spouse. The facts were the facts. She used to be with me, but then she moved on to be with someone else. As the ex, I only had one option, and that was to get over it. I am not trying to make something very difficult seem very easy. Far from it. But clearly the relationship we had was changed, and now we needed to find a completely different relationship going forward. I needed to find a different vantage point from which to view her and us.

We weren't husband and wife anymore, duh. But we weren't just friends either. We were so much more than that. We were richer and deeper than friends. And so how to frame that best became the question that needed answers.

Here's the answer that I came up with. I wanted to let the relationship between us become bigger than very best friends but lesser than spouses, and the key that best fit in the lock was that we become…*Siblings*! You read that right, siblings, aka brother and sister. Me, the older brother. Her, the kid sister. Under that canopy, I could still love her, root for her, share ideas and problems with her, raise the kids with her. I could be completely open about almost everything, as one would be with a sibling. She was still in my life and very close to me, but now on a completely different basis. The relationship was not over, but the paradigm that governed it had shifted. I had to let go of the woman who had been my wife and welcome the woman who would become my sister. Since I never actually had a sister, she was my first, and I welcomed having her in that role.

As templates go, it worked perfectly and continues to work perfectly to this day. Knowing that she was never going to be romantic with me again allowed me to set her free, to let her go forever, to let her become this other person in my heart. Since we weren't ever again going to bed together, the whole metric of boy-girl tension was out the window. There was no flirting, no batting eyes, no nothing. We achieved a new balance and moved forward into our future as brother and sister. We're still doing it that way, and it's still working.

So in your own situation, if you are going to have a good divorce, you have to let your spouse go, and with her or him goes the relationship you had together. That one is changed forever, and a new one has to emerge; a new relationship has to take its place. For me it was like we became siblings. Older brother and younger sister. Yours may become like mine. Or it may become a version of it, like your ex is the older sister, and you are the younger brother. Whatever it is, try to find it. It may take a year to figure out what works best for you, but I include this concept to say that you can be creative and figure it out for yourself. You are not locked into any metric or any guideline. Whatever works for you is what you're after. Your new relationship with your ex should only be what brings you both the most peace and happiness. If the ex doesn't want to be close to you, then you won't be close. Sorry, case closed. But, if he or she does want an ongoing friendship, the sibling gambit may work for you too.

Whatever the new relationship is, use it to encourage each other to become your new selves. Whoever and whomever that might be. You don't know who you two will become, and neither does your spouse. The story has yet to be written. Men, encourage your ex to keep her heart innocent and her will to love again intact. Be gracious and kind to her always. Be giving and generous. Now and forever. Like there's no other choice. Women, encourage your ex to a new kind of greatness. One that uses the relationship that has just ended as a platform to whatever is next in his life. Try to do nothing that holds him back from it. Encourage each other in all the things you are both trying to do, especially new things. This will let you both become someone different in each other's lives. Having a new workable relationship with the person who used to be your best friend might become one of the great benefits of your good divorce.

Things to Avoid Doing, Whatever Else You Do

1. *Criticizing Your Ex*

    For now and for the foreseeable future, avoid leveling any criticisms at your ex, no matter how deserved they may be. You lost the right to stand in judgment when the marriage ended. If you have something you want to say, and it's not nice, write it down, think about it for a few days, and then throw that piece of paper away. It probably won't matter that much a few days later anyway. Whatever wisdom you have to share, find the nicest possible way to present it, long before you present it. If you are upset about something that has been done or said—which you will be at some point, I guarantee—try to swallow your pride and swallow your words. Just keep your unkind thoughts to yourself. Do not text them, email them, Facebook them, etc. Keep a journal of insults you can just burn later.

    Your ex should get the same kind of kid glove treatment as your boss. End of story. No criticisms.

2. *Criticizing Your Ex's Next*

    Your ex is going to fall in love again. With someone, sometime. They always do. And maybe it's already happened, maybe it will happen this afternoon. Here's some news—nobody cares what you think on this subject. When it comes to your ex and the next, you really have nothing to say. Your opinions are not required. No need to share any of them, especially with your ex, your mutual friends or your children or anyone else in your Rolodex. Please just keep them to yourself.

The only exception to this guideline would be if you have something nice to say about this person, and in that case, share as much as you like.

3. *Flirting*

Not sure why it happens, but newly divorced people get way too flirty and frisky with the rest of the population. For some reason, once all the papers are filed, and the new life is underway, they get into that mindset. Possibly it is all the new-found freedom. Possibly they are going to parties and receptions on their own for the first time in a long time. Possibly they are spending too much time alone and have started to think that everything they think up is hilarious. Or maybe it's just social anxiety. But for whatever reason, flirting happens.

But you don't have to follow that lead. Save yourself and the rest of us the embarrassment. It's kinda like bad breath and just as hard to tell someone about it. No Flirting.

4. *Flaunting*

You will fall in love again. Life goes on, and your heart will lead the way. It's inevitable. And once you do strike up something new, I encourage you to enjoy it and wrap yourself in it and thrill to every minute of it. But, but, but... This new situation should be discreet, especially in the beginning, and even more especially around your kids and ex. So you got a new boyfriend or girlfriend, great! Look at you! It's not like you opened a restaurant or climbed Mount Whitney. You got a new boyfriend or girlfriend. That's it and that's all. No good reason whatsoever to parade around and flaunt your new happiness before the world at large. That would be weaponizing the new arrangements. Especially since this person will undoubtedly be younger than your ex, though hopefully older than your children.

If a new situation is just a *fling*, i.e. a nothing, it's nobody's business but your own anyway. In the beginning, in any case. If it turns into a real relationship, there will be plenty of time to tell everyone. No Flaunting.

The Dividends of a Good Divorce

First dividend: A Lady in the Rain—As our divorce was rounding the final turn and headed down the home stretch, I was looking at the past darkly and at the future with dread. I hadn't been alone in almost twenty years. I was comfortable and happy in my beautiful house. I loved my neighborhood and my neighbors. And I knew all of this was going to change. A friend asked me if I was in another relationship yet, and I recall telling him, quite truthfully, that I was not and that it was probably the very last thing on my list of things to do. The very last thing. After a root canal. And having my colon scraped. I was still living with my ex and the boys, but by this time, I was in the study downstairs while she slept upstairs. It was clearly an untenable situation that spoke of the many changes coming very soon in all of our lives. Mine more than anyone else's obviously.

On the way home one night from work, it started to rain, and the wind started to howl. And by the time I got near my house, it was a sideways rain blowing across the windshield as the wipers swiped hopelessly. I pulled into a gas station. Filling up my car, I noticed a woman walking out of the office of the gas station with one of those red plastic gas cans. She had no umbrella and started walking up the muddy street. About one hundred feet away, I saw a pair of emergency lights blinking weakly through the downpour. She had run out of gas within a pitching wedge of the gas station, and the penalty was already severe. She was drenched, alone, and being ignored by the hundreds of cars going by. There under the canopy, I was very dry as I filled up my own tank and watched as she walked through the mud and tried to get some of the gas from the little red plastic can into her empty tank.

I was already a few minutes late but could not leave someone so helpless in a situation so miserable. I pulled out of the gas station and went back the way I came and made a U-turn, pulling my car up behind hers. I tried to help but the plastic can's nozzle clearly did not fit her car, and gas was spilling all over both of us and all over the wet street. I suggested that she get in my car and let me drive her the one hundred feet to the gas station. She hesitated but said okay, and we drove back. I called AAA and asked them to send a truck for her, with lots of gas in it, and I bought her a cup of coffee and gave her one of my dry golf jackets, plus twenty dollars as a gratuity for the driver. It was a complete rescue. I went home and had dinner with everyone and did not give it that much thought.

About a week later, I got a box of cookies as a thank you. And few days after that, she stopped by my office to return the jacket and say thank you in person. The woman who I met in the lobby of my office that day looked nothing like the drowned and soaking wet figure I had helped in the rain. In fact, she was pretty beautiful, and I almost got tongue-tied, but thank goodness I didn't. After about twenty minutes of chit-chat, she said, "Well, I guess that's it." And she started to go.

Out of nowhere, I said, "A lot of things had to happen for us to meet… The rain, the gas, both of us on that street at that moment in time… Maybe we're supposed to know each other."

She looked at me oddly and asked me what I was asking of her. I said maybe we could see some music together or have dinner or something simple like that, just friends. I added that I had two sons who were more important to me than anything in the world, and that I was separated from my wife.

She said, "I'm also separated."

I got a big smile on my face and said, "See there, maybe we *are* supposed to know each other."

A few weeks later, we saw a show and then had dinner, and then started seeing each other more and more, again and again. *We have been together ever since.* We have never had a fight or even an argument worth mentioning. She is my peace, she is my light, she is my everything. And thank goodness we found each other. A new relationship was the last thing I was looking for, the last thing I ever expected to find, and despite that, somehow I was willing and open to the possibility that fate would come tumbling into my life. Fate put one of the great loves I will ever know right in front of me, in the person of a lady in the rain.

I share this story because it is a direct result of my good divorce. My ex was my counselor throughout this adventure. I hadn't dated anyone in twenty years, and she was the one I confided in and discussed love strategies with. She knew me better than anyone on the planet at the time and gave me great advice on how to proceed in the love affair that was overtaking me. She wasn't jealous or resentful. She was full of positive energy and great suggestions.

Because of the good divorce that we were in the middle of, she had no reason not to be anything but amazing. I had been upfront and honest with her about everything, and generous too of course, so there were no lingering resentments or tragic memories to dwell on. As I mentioned earlier, she was slipping into her new role in my life as my kid sister anyway. And she took her new responsibilities toward me quite seriously. Her ideas helped me at every turn, and because of her guidance, I was able to start the relationship that has become my greatest love.

Second dividend: A Doctor to Save My Life—I was attending my twenty-eighth South by Southwest Conference (SXSW). This is a five-day get-together that brings music executives of all strips and stripes together with literally thousands of musicians, there looking for affiliations with a record company, a management firm, a music publisher, an agent, a merch company, whatever. It is one of the highlights of the music business calendar, and aside from the great food and camaraderie and all that amazing music, Austin, Texas, is a great place to spend a long weekend.

During the course of the Saturday afternoon, I noticed a heaviness developing in my legs. It was completely unexplainable. I had not just run a marathon or done a hundred squats, but the muscles in my legs felt like it. They ached like I had been beaten with a stick. Then by Sunday morning, I could barely get out of bed and struggled to make my flight back to Los Angeles. The next morning after that, I knew something was terribly wrong. I was unable to get out of bed or up from the john and could barely dress myself. It was as though my muscles were no longer working.

Dr. Ron looked me over a few hours later and suggested I check into the hospital immediately.

He said, "You have something, but I'm not sure what it is. Might be anything."

He covered his mouth with a handy facemask and covered his hands with antibacterial liquid. An hour later, I checked into Little Company of Mary Hospital in Torrance, California. Panicked. Terrified.

But there in the emergency room, I realized I was in great hands. My ex-brother-in-law, Dr. John, was chief of staff at that hospital. Despite the fact that his sister and I had just divorced, Dr. John assured me that he would personally look after me. And he did. He took care of me like I was the president of the United States. Everything I needed, I got. Every test, every expert, every possibility of how to discover what was wrong with me was explored. He knew that the sooner they could figure out what was going on with me, the sooner the treatment could begin, and the sooner I would get better. Within about eight hours, I had a brain scan, a spinal tap, a full-body MRI, a CT scan, a complete panel of blood work, a chest X-ray, and a couple of other things that probed me in ways I hope never to be probed again. Everyone was very polite and respectful.

One of the nurses, a technician, trying to reassure me, told me they were just trying to rule out some of the many possibilities. I asked, "What possibilities are those?"

He said, "They just want to make sure you don't have something really bad, like adult polio or brain cancer or anything like that."

What the?

I thought maybe I had a bad flu or something like that. But wait, now they were trying to rule out things like cancer? I was beginning the long slow descent into complete mental chaos when Dr. John appeared to see how everything was going. He seemed calm and at ease and put me at ease as well. He confirmed that they were ruling out the most terrible possibilities and that they should have an answer by later that night or first thing in the morning. He must have seen the look on my face and so started to reassure me that everything would be okay. He said he suspected that I might have something called Guillain-Barre (pronounced Gee-On Burr-Ray) syndrome. It's an autoimmune disease. Your immune system attacks your nervous system and shuts down your body's ability to control your muscles.

He gave me a squeeze on the shoulder and a smile and said, "But we'll know much more in the morning after all the tests come back."

Researching this disease I had never even heard of before, I learned that the author Joseph Heller had it, as did Franklin Delano Roosevelt, and that it ruined both their lives. Sufferers can often spend months or years in intensive care and live the rest of their lives in a diminished fashion. Well, then, I thought, so this is it. This is how I'm going out.

I lay there, in my hospital bed, thinking of a number of things. First that I was faced with impossible futures. One with brain cancer, one with adult polio, or one with a disease

I had never even heard of before. Second, how sad my new wife had sounded on the phone when I called to give her an update on my condition. She was crying as she gave our boy a bath. And third, how glad I was that the doctor guiding me through this particular street of hell was my children's Uncle Johnny, my dear brother-in-law—yes, my ex-brother-in-law, whatever—and I was so incredibly thankful that the breakup with his sister was as sane and peaceful as it had been. By ensuring and fighting for a good and kind divorce, it allowed him to be there with me, helping me, saving my life.

I heard myself saying over and over, "Please let it be Guillain-Barre. Please let it be Guillain-Barre." I didn't really know what it was, but I knew it couldn't be as bad as the brain cancer and adult polio. I wept myself to sleep.

The next morning, it was confirmed—Guillain-Barre. And if not caught early, it can kill you. Or doctors put you in a forced coma until your body can recover a working knowledge of its nerve endings. Its victims often need canes or walkers. But this was not to be my fate. Thanks to Dr. John, the hospital staff worked like superstars and very quickly and diligently processed the results of all my tests almost immediately. Thanks to them and him, it was all caught in time. They were able to stop the downward slide of my health instantly. The treatment began that morning with the first of three bottles a day of gamma globulin, which reset my immune system and redefined its purpose. The disease was less than four days into its conquest of my body when they began the treatment that would reverse its effects completely and altogether and forever.

By the next morning, Wednesday, I was already much improved. I could actually get out of bed to answer the knock on my door. Thursday morning, I was prowling the hallways a little. Friday morning, I was helping other patients with their meals and walking those who needed a walk. Saturday morning came, and I was ready to go home but needed three more bottles of that sweet elixir in my system. Sunday morning, I checked out. It was such an unbelievable feeling to walk, unaided, a little gingerly, mind you, but walking nonetheless, out of that hospital. Some people get that disease and never walk again, their lives compromised forever.

But not me! I was free of all that pain and sorrow and back on track within just a few days. It was unbelievable. Had it not been for Dr. John and his willingness to make me his priority, treating me like I was still his brother, putting all the resources of the hospital to the test, and giving me the quickest route to find a cure, my life would have been ruined.

The fact that Dr. John was there for me, to that extent and to that degree, helping me turn one of the most difficult moments in my life into just a close call, was not the intended product of my respectful and gentle divorce from his sister. But it was an unintended consequence. His presence was proof that I had handled things the right way, not only for my ex but for her whole family. I was not a pariah, I was not a scourge, I was not an outcast. I was someone who had loved their daughter and sister and made all the sacrifices required to allow her to continue to have a beautiful life after I was no longer her husband.

My good divorce had provided another dividend—it literally saved my life.

Third dividend: A Team to Find a New Home—This is an absolutely a true story, in spite of how unusual it might seem. Right after my ex and I had resolved everything and signed all the papers, there was still the little matter of where I was going to live. By this time, I had met my beautiful new wife, the woman I hope will spend the rest of her life with me. Some medical miracles had transpired, including her fighting two cancers, and as a result, we were blessed to be the parents of our boy, my third son. He was about one. We decided we wanted to live near the other boys so that there could be lots of interactions and family time.

My ex-wife's mom, my ex-mother-in-law, agreed to be our real estate agent, and she had found a few places she thought we might like to look at. So picture this: We decided to go as a big group to look at the open houses. I was driving. Sitting next to me in the passenger seat was my now-ex-wife. Sitting behind me was my now ex-mother-in-law. Next to her was my new wife, and next to her was my new son. All very cozy and friendly. At every one of the four open houses, we followed the same routine. I pulled the car up to the front, and *the three women jumped out* to see if the house was right for me and my new circumstances. That's right, *all three of them*. My new boy wasn't quite speaking yet, so I felt free to turn to him and remark, "Can you believe this? All of them running around, helping us find a place to live!" He picked his nose in acknowledgement and went about making a wreck of my new car.

Presently the three women would exit the house and walk back to the car, their assessments at the ready.

"Not big enough," one would say.

"No view at all," said another.

"The kitchen needs remodeling," said my ex-mother-in-law. And so it went all afternoon. At least four different houses suffered their collective reviews. And all the while, I felt like the luckiest man in the world. These three women were taking time out of their lives and homes in order to help me find a home for me and my life and loves. There was no animosity, no jealousy, no anger at all among anyone. It had all worked.

Ultimately my wife and I did find our dream house. And as a further example of divorcing well, my ex-mother-in-law was our real estate agent, and wow, was she tremendous. She covered every detail, arranged every meeting and inspection, and brought her complete passion to the task at hand, despite the fact that her daughter and I had divorced some years before. She was still my mother-in-law, and I was still her son-in-law. It was all good.

How was this overflowing of goodwill even possible? Here's how, I think. Because I had made every effort to make sure that it happened like that. I was generous and respectful of my ex and her family throughout the marriage and the divorce. I took a long time realizing that I was going to have to get a divorce, and then a further long time letting the idea develop into something, and then meticulously planned how to exit with the least amount of damage to all the relationships hanging in the balance. I did not have a messy ending and embarrass myself or anyone who loved me.

That day, looking for a new house, stands out in my mind as the ultimate and everlasting proof that I had achieved what I had set out to do: I had a good divorce. Wife, ex-wife, and ex-mother-in-law, all hanging out together, in the close confines of my car, along with my new son. Their willingness to help me was like a medal of valor on my chest, a braid on my shoulder that told the world what kind of guy I was and what kind of things I had survived to get there. Regardless of the journey that put us all in the same car at the same time, sharing the same purpose, at that moment, we were a family of sorts, a modern family, moving forward into its uncharted future, one open house at a time. Yet another dividend, this one with interest, of my good divorce.

Celebrating Your Past with Your Ex

I believe in this concept, and I live it. As you build a new relationship with your ex, post-divorce, you can still reach out. Maybe it's a birthday or Mother's Day or Father's Day or the anniversary of your first date or the kids' birthdays or whatever it is. Possibly this sounds ridiculous to some of you, but don't shoot the messenger. It has worked for me and continues to work for me. My ex and I might have a laugh recalling something funny that happened at the wedding or something frightening that happened on the honeymoon, or relive the chill from the almost-car-accident on the way to her parents' fiftieth that would have changed everything forever.

We are simply remembering and reminding each other of all the shared treasure of all those years together. It's a small thing, remembering our past, but it's a huge thing too. By continuing to celebrate our shared experiences, we are honoring our time together, reminiscing about the friends we were way back when.

My Wife and My Ex SoulCycle Together, Among Other Things

Yes, you read that correctly. And it's true. They call each other, mention the class time they are taking, and often even ride next to each other. I am not worried at all about what they might say about me when they are together. One might say I *am* a great husband, and the other might say I *was* a great husband. Or one might say that I'm putting on a little weight or need to floss more or whatever. They are not besties, but they are pals. They have a common experience that unites them, which is obviously me and that both of them married me. But that they know each other well enough to hang out and exercise together on occasion is further proof of concept of a good divorce.

The fact of their friendship underscores the success of my efforts to leave my marriage well and stay close and friendly with my ex and her whole family. The fact that we can also get together for Thanksgiving and Christmas is the reward I get for any sacrifices I made, financial or otherwise, during the divorce.

It was always my goal to end the marriage the right way, by being generous, negotiating kindly, leaving lovingly, returning someday and staying friends forever. Someday is now every day.

CHAPTER 5

Others' Stories

There is something to be said about learning from those who walk ahead down a difficult path. They offer much knowledge just being there. Like a Sherpa. Looking at it from a Darwinian standpoint, experiential learning is key to our survival as a species. Only by watching the primates in the next tree do something brilliant (or not brilliant) did we learn to do, or not to do, the same thing. It is no less true in humans now as it was in bonobos then. What follows here are the details of several different situations, some disasters and some successes. These are stories of the lives that were changed forever by the facts and fates and decisions made before, during, and after a divorce.

Divorced His Wife Three Times

This is the story of Larry and what he went through to get divorced from his wife, once and for all. It took him three tries. Not because he married her three separate times, he only married her once. But he could not get away from her. It turned out that the prenup they signed had a couple of gaping holes through which millions of his dollars were headed. Three separate court appearances, three separate sets of interrogatories, three separate sets of depositions, and several non-court proceedings. There were not just three separate sets of attorneys he had to pay for. There were actually *six* sets of attorneys because the original prenup stated that he would pay for her lawyers, in the "unlikely" event that their nuptials were to end in a divorce. So imagine that. Larry was not only paying for his own lawyers but also the lawyers who were suing him on behalf of his ex-wife. He was paying guys to kick his ass *and* take his money.

His strategy in the beginning was to fight like hell and give her as little as possible, make her grind for every penny, and pay her back. This was probably because he married a woman he loved and gave her everything she needed to be happy, which she just could not find a way to be. The divorce wasn't his doing. He wanted them to go to therapy and work everything out, and it appeared that she just wanted out.

In no time at all, they were in front of a judge who was only too happy to divorce them. But she soon realized that she couldn't live on $7,900 a month while still trying to take care of the kids and start her new business and pay for her boyfriends to travel with her all over the world. So she sued him again to get it up to $9,500 a month, plus increases in child support and a sizeable investment in her new business. That was divorce 2. That kept things quiet for a little while, but soon enough, divorce 2 was not working either. When she found out she was supposed to pay for the children's tuition out of *her* share, divorce 3 appeared on the horizon. How could she live in the custom to which she had grown accustomed being married to him if she had to pay for expensive private school as well? So she sued him again. Divorce 3.

The third divorce was just as bloody as the first two. Filled with reliable tropes. Full of anger and disdain, they described each other in plain and certain language as deceivers and withholders of information and truth. They *really* went after each other on this one. Her lawyers gave it their best, but he protected himself pretty well. He kept his house, she has to rent, and there will be a moment in time when he does not have to write her any more checks either. But they learned to despise each other and hardly spoke at all for several years.

Like in a championship fight, divorce is one of those things where you have to protect yourself at all times. The reason we have contracts between each other is not for the good days, it is for the not-so-good days. A comma here and a comma there can make all the difference between you and your money. But it should never have to get to the point as described above. Larry did not play the game well enough. He was making lots of money, and certainly she was entitled to a good portion of it, but he fought her tooth and nail in the beginning, and this came back to haunt him. There would have been no need for these two situations to get so completely out of control if he had simply been more generous in the first place. He lowballed her and paid the price.

The Wisdom—Be as generous as you possibly can be! Do not use the divorce to punish your spouse. If Larry (not his real name) had been more giving in the first divorce, he would have likely avoided the two additional ones.

He certainly thinks that now.

Bought His Ex's Boyfriend a Castle

This is the story of paying guilt money and how that can ruin a life. And the story of a perfect storm that swept an otherwise very nice guy right into a river of debt and over a waterfall of idiocy. It was bad luck, bad timing, and a number of bad decisions that put him in a hole from which there was no digging out.

This divorce starts in England where Stevie, my friend, a very successful promoter and artist manager, did something stupid that a lot of guys do. Right in the middle of his working marriage, he started having an affair with his secretary, which grew into more and more complications and, finally, became a real relationship. He felt terribly guilty about the whole situation and decided to tell his wife, ask for a divorce, and give her much more than the courts would have required that he give her. He was trying to make up for things he did not do well by doing something he should never have done. He was on top of the world at that point, making a lot of money, and there was no reason to think it would stop. He was so sure that the rest of his life would be as sweet as that which preceded it, that he did not take into account the vagaries of fate and karma. And thus, he completely ruined everything.

The divorce moved ahead, and after much handwring-ing and self-loathing, he decided to give the wife the small castle he had purchased and they had refurbished with his bil-lowingly large income. Small, but still a castle! Many rooms, some acreage, and tons of prestige, seeing that it had been the former tryst site of an English king many years before. So drenched in guilt that he had been unfaithful and destroyed his otherwise lovely marriage, he tried to get over it by being overly and unnecessarily generous to his wife. She did noth-ing to stop him, and who can blame her. The more she shut up, the more she got.

Meanwhile Stevie and the former-secretary-now-girl-friend established residence at a lovely little three-bedroom flat near the castle so they could be near the kids and so that everyone could stay friends. Stevie had in mind that he would still be part of his old family's life, so why not live close enough to drop by, he reasoned. She was okay with it too. And as happens, the ex-wife found someone new. A man very much younger than the husband, and being a broke musician, someone always on the lookout for a good practice space and an opportunity to move up the social ladder in any way one can. And in the ex-wife, he found both. Although he knew of the husband, he had no respect for the quaint idea of the ex-husband hanging around all that much any-way. Within a few months, he moved into the castle. One thing led to another, as they always do, and one particular night, the boyfriend and the ex-wife were drinking and par-tying way too much, and she slipped on one of the enormous staircases and tumbled down them, banging her head so hard that she went into a coma—*from which she would never wake up*! After a year, they decided to pull the plug, and that was that. Life over. All terribly sad, and all precipitated by Stevie being unable to keep various bits of his anatomy to himself. But what about the castle, you might want to ask?

Since the castle represented roughly twice the financial equivalent of thirty years of alimony and child support, all rolled into one huge bundle, Stevie knocked on the door and told the boyfriend to pack up his belongings and get the hell out. He had no intention of seeing the boyfriend end up with the thirty years of benefits that were intended solely for the ex-wife and the kids. As you can imagine, the boyfriend laughed in his face, slammed the door, and hired a lawyer. The boyfriend sued the estate and claimed that since he and the ex-wife were living together (even though it had only been a few months before she fell down the stairs), he had established residency with her, and the structure of a relationship was in place. And since there was no will, and since he was the nearest thing to being a spouse, he argued that the place was his. Through some insane travesty of justice, the courts agreed that a relationship was in place and *awarded the boyfriend the castle*!

By this time, Stevie's lucrative businesses had turned themselves into much more modest endeavors. This was most likely because trends in music and film had changed during the process of the breakup and divorce, and Stevie did not keep his eye on those trends. Thus he could no longer afford the luxury of several lawyers and multiple courts to get his property back, and so he had no choice but to accept the injustice that life had delivered to him. He drove by his old castle every day and was required for years to ask the boyfriend's permission to visit his own children there. It was a combination of the very worst of all the possible outcomes. In an equally pitiful development, the secretary/girlfriend grew tired of witnessing his misery. She, being young and having no qualms about anything at all, actually started up a relationship with the musician, now a landowner, and within a year's time, she also moved into the castle.

Yes, this is absolutely the worst divorce story of all time.

The Wisdom—Guilt for one's transgressions has no place or value in the transactions of a divorce proceeding. You cannot possibly make up for anything that happened in the marriage by being overly generous in the divorce. No purpose in mixing the emotions of your situation with the business of it. There is a canyon of value between generosity and noble stupidity, and poor Stevie fell right in it. Be generous, yes, but not ridiculous. You never know what's going to happen.

Finally Told the Truth

Once you know your relationship is ending—and this can become known to you through a thousand flickering lights or one blazing inferno—the actual exit must have planning and forethought. Plan your exit as well as you planned your entrance. The following story is about someone I knew about, who did nothing right, ended things badly, and paid dearly for it.

He was married for twenty-plus years and was, by then, several years into an affair. Like many men in this situation, once things got started, there was no way to stop once the awkward balance had been achieved. Next thing he knew, years had gone by, and a child had been borne to him by his mistress. Sooner or later, as they always do, everything goes public, and he found out that there was going to be a big public exposé of his life and particularly the affair and the child. A front-page story on all the gossip rags was imminent. So he decided he needed to tell his wife, if for no other reason than to save her a little embarrassment. Very late in the game to be thinking about his wife and her embarrassment, but that's the way it went down. I'm not judging here, just reporting. But in addition to all that, he decided the best way to handle the delivery of the news was over the phone. Yet another one of his terrible ideas, but there you go. His assistant got the wife on the phone, and the slippery slope became an Olympic ski run.

He said, "I have some news." Long pause. "I wanted to let you know that I am going to be on the front page of the paper—tomorrow."

"For something good, I hope?" she posited.

"No," he replied.

"Oh my god. What have you done?" she said.

"I meant to tell you earlier, but it's about an affair."

Aghast would not even begin to explain her reaction. "WHAT DID YOU SAY? YOU HAD AN AFFAIR? You lying bastard…"

He gave her a moment to calm down.

She asked, "I suppose it's been going on for just a short time?"

He steeled himself for her reaction. "Actually no, it's been going on for quite some time. Several years, in fact."

She was apoplectic. "SEVERAL YEARS? DID YOU SAY YEARS? You are quite the bastard, aren't you?"

"I thought you should know, and that's why I'm telling you."

"You should have told me about this years ago, when I could have done something to save our relationship and not spent the last however many years out here with all our friends and family…LIVING A LIE!"

"Yes, I understand." He threw that out like an under-sized life preserver.

She breathed deeply a couple of times.

He continued, "There's more."

She slammed the phone onto a nearby counter. "What more could there be?"

After a long pause, he said, "There's a child."

"Oh, you LYING AWFUL BASTARD. A CHILD! You're just going to rot in hell when it's all said and done, aren't you?" She paused to catch her breath. "I suppose the child was just born, and that's why the news is coming out now?"

Again he readied for her reaction. "Actually no. She's about to turn nine."

"ABOUT TO TURN NINE? WHAT HAVE YOU BEEN DOING ALL THESE YEARS? Oh, you are one lying stinking bastard to have kept this from me and OUR children..."

He delivered the final blow. "The kids actually know her. They've known her for years. They just don't know she's mine."

"OH, YOU ARE THE MOST AWFUL LYING BASTARD THE WORLD HAS EVER SEEN, YOU MISERABLE SCUM..." She went on for several minutes.

And there it was, his sad truth laid bare for all to see. Told over the phone. The wife almost lost her mind hearing these final details and made the decision that she would make him pay—and pay significantly—for all the grief and sadness and deception that he had just brought to her life. And she did, giving her one of the biggest settlements in that country's lengthy list of expensive divorces.

He made many mistakes. But he wasn't thinking clearly and clearly had not been thinking clearly for the last however many years. He hurt his wife and did so over a decade or more. So when she had the chance, she hurt him back and made him pay dearly for every ounce of angst he caused her. Because he was wealthy, he had to pay a very high price for his divorce anyway, but then almost like the punitive phase of a wrongful death trial, the ex-wife wanted some blood money too. And because she was so pissed off and so ashamed that he had taken so long to tell her, she made sure he never forgot how much he hurt her.

He should not have had the affair or the child or any of the rest of it. But things happen in life, and not all of them are positive. The affair was a mistake, yes, and the length of it was almost a crime, yes, but he gained a child, and when it was all over, he married his mistress. Everyone has forgiven him except the ex, who has gone on to have several additional relationships and has not found happiness in any one of them, at least not yet.

The Wisdom—When you know the relationship is finished and completely over, the person you married has the right to know that. Almost as soon as you know it. You need not share every tawdry detail of how and why and when and for how long you've been lying, but you definitely need to say that it's over, as soon as *you* know it's over. Several years is ridiculous, and it will cost you dearly. Only the immediate truth will allow you to set the stage for a good divorce.

Married a Nightmare

Don Scranton was one of the most gracious and gentle gentlemen I had ever met or known in my entire life. He had the build of Justin Timberlake, the wit of Steve Martin, and the grace of a lifelong ballroom dancer. He loved to golf and listen to music and to sit down with a friend and a martini and wile away an afternoon. The reason for all the tranquility in his life was the fact the he loved quiet. His conversations were tidy and neat, what little anger he ever displayed was done in a whisper, and he would greet controversy with a wry smile. Everything about him was soft-spoken. He was not a flashy dresser. His house was clean and simple. And he was the one who would say, "You go ahead and tell your story. I'll tell mine later." And then listen to you until you were done.

We were having lunch once, and somehow the topic rolled around to which of us had made bigger and stupider mistakes in our lives. So there we were, exchanging stories. I told him how I unintentionally insulted Shirley Temple Black at a State Dinner in front of the Prime Minister of Italy. He laughed at the very idea of such a thing and then said, "Did I ever tell you about the first woman I married?" And out comes his story. As quiet as he was, the first wife was the opposite. She told big stories, she had big hair, she had a big laugh. Everything he was, she was not. But somehow, they saw a future in each other, and she loved him a lot, or so it appeared, and he thought he could learn to live with the "bigness" of her (his air quotes) that were not exactly to his taste.

So they got married, and of course, it was a big wedding. Hundreds of friends and even a big band. Like I said, everything about this woman was big. They were two years and one small baby into the marriage when a fight broke out. She was mad as hell about something. I can tell you that Don did not start it nor did anything to continue it but was simply trying to protect himself at that point because he never had fights with anyone. He treasured his quiet. The wife then started to scream at him. At the top of her voice, high-pitched sounds that were barely words were coming out of her mouth, full of anger and vitriol and suspicion, and it wouldn't stop. She was like a teakettle that someone forgot to turn off. She went on for what felt like almost ten minutes, or so he recalled. All directed at him, who stood there, blinking at her like a fish looking out of his bowl, unsure what to do next and still not even sure what was unfolding before him. This man loved nothing more than quiet after all.

At our lunch, many years later, he told me that he knew *that instant* that the marriage was finished. He knew that he could never let his guard down around her, ever again. The marriage had been assassinated. Despite his wisdom and grace and understanding of the world, and a legion of friends to give him advice and counsel, he had made the worst decision of his life and married his worst nightmare, that being a screamer. But he turned his disaster around by getting the hell out of there as soon as he could. He arranged for the divorce to be handled as quickly and simply as possible, with a minimum of fuss and bother, without any yelling or screaming, so to speak. Probably paid more than he had to in alimony and child support, but he did not care. He knew that he never wanted to hear the sound of her screaming again ever for the rest of his life. *E-V-E-R.*

Don handled his business the way it should be handled in that situation. He left the wife, paid the bill and wrote the big check, and never thought to look back. She was a neutral party in his life going forward, neither friend nor foe, and that was just fine with him. Although he hated the idea of divorce, he hated the idea of being married to her even more. So he did what he had to do. She may have never known exactly why he left, and he told me he never told her exactly why either. She remarried, he remarried, and that was that.

I ran into the son many, many years later and told him how much I loved his dad and that he had set an example for me on how to be a gentleman in a difficult situation. The son had no idea what broke up his parents. And he never will.

The Wisdom—Part of the mechanism of a divorce is timing, recognizing when you are not supposed to be married to a particular person any longer. Sometimes it takes decades, sometimes it's a weekend, and in the case of my friend Don Scranton (not his real name by the way), it took less than ten minutes. But once realized, you have to get out. You have to get out and get yourself free so your humanity will not be diminished any more than it is already. Act fast, do the right thing, handle the business of your divorce fairly, with respect, and get to what's next.

Got Divorced Before He Got Married

My friend Al was single with no children. He owned a successful investment firm which had been up and running for twenty years or more. He was not looking to get married or even get into an extended relationship, but so much for plans. He met a woman with a couple of kids, and they all moved in together. As with most givers, Al was very attracted to takers. As with most takers, Jacki was very attracted to Al. And so it happened that Al found himself in a relationship with someone who saw every opportunity with him as another possibility for her gain. He gave and she took, over and over. Most givers don't realize they keep falling for takers, and most takers know this and keep looking for givers who are only too willing to fall for them.

Al helped her with the taxes, he helped her with the car, he helped her with her business, and by helped, I mean he paid for things. Then they got engaged. Alarms went off among his group of friends of which I am a part. Fun is fun, but an engagement was way too serious. Wasn't it too sudden? Does he really know her like that? What the hell is he thinking? But our dear friend was not to be dissuaded. He had been waiting for the right woman for a long time, and she was pretty close. Close enough anyway.

As a prewedding gift, he even moved their residence from the beach to the hills and bought a house that she loved much more than he did. Watching him cater to her was like watching someone driving and texting and heading right for a cliff. But he did one very wise thing. He refused to commit to a wedding date. There was something about that last step that was making him wary and ultimately keeping him at bay. Without a finish line, his fiancée began to grow more urgent and reckless and pushy and demanding. Some might say she changed under the pressure, others might say she simply revealed herself under the pressure. She also became envious and suspicious and would greet him at the door with a hundred questions about what he did that day and with whom, and ask why didn't he call her to tell her and all the rest of it.

Within a few months of his evading the final detail, all that giving reached a natural conclusion, and Al started to look around and ask, quite naturally, "Well, what about me?"

By this time, she was in such the habit of taking and disguising it as loving that there was really nothing for her to give him. It was like he had been standing in a room that just ran out of air, and he could not breathe. So Al did a very practical thing on behalf of himself and the rest of his life. He stopped everything. Broke up with her and ended the relationship. It didn't matter that he had already cosigned for her car, paid for her child's tuition at private school, and bought a house he didn't even like that much. Enough was enough. He was done, and he stopped the train. There would be no divorce because there would be no marriage. He regarded the money he had already spent as the price of the lessons he had learned. Life lessons. One thing he had learned from investing, don't throw good money after bad.

He walked away from that situation with his head held high, his heart unmarked, and his credit rating unblemished. Was it awkward? I bet it was. Was it uncomfortable? I imagine so. But was it the absolute right thing to do? *Abso-you-betcha-lutely*! Instead of putting himself in a situation that would drain him, he cut his losses and got the hell out. He got divorced *before* he got married. He wrote a couple of checks, paid for her moving expenses, removed his name from anything having to do with her and her lousy credit rating, and got out with no obligations. And he let her keep the ring too. Smart man!

The Wisdom—Follow your instinct, protect yourself, handle your business, and get out if you realize that a relationship will never have a chance to succeed.

Got Completely Carried Away

Hector was a great composer, conductor, author, and bon vivant, whose extreme passions often brought him face-to-face with agony. During his adult lifetime, he lived in Paris, at least from medical school on to the end. This is the story of his marriage to someone who should have remained his muse but whom he tried to turn into his wife. It took place many years ago but applies to these times with uncanny relevance.

When he was a young man in his late twenties, Hector attended a visiting English theater company's performance of a Shakespeare play and saw, for the first time, a woman named Harriet. He fell completely and totally in love with her. He wrote to her many times that he had never seen such a face or heard such a beautiful voice and that his heart belonged to her from the first glimpse. She did not pay him much attention because it was just fan mail, and his English was not so amazing. Realizing what he was up against, he knew that he needed to find a way to tell her how much he loved her in a language they could both understand. So he came up with a novel idea. He let his love for her become one of the inspirations for a symphony. It was his way of saying what his words could not. It tells, musically, the story of a man's quest on the journey of his life. It is one of the great symphonic works of that era, in fact, a masterpiece for the ages. His love for this woman helped him create one of his life's great works. And if that's where the story ended, it would be great, but you know how men are. Never leave well enough alone. Never leave the stone unturned. Never quite know when to stop. Always trying to get a little more water out of the well.

Once his symphony was finished, Hector arranged to have it performed in Paris and asked Mademoiselle Harriet to attend the concert. She couldn't make it. He kept on with the letters and flowers and even got an apartment near her so he could watch her come and go. Some would call this stalking, but this was the 1830's after all. He never forgot her, is the point, when maybe he should have considered doing so.

Two years later, the symphony was performed again, and this time, she was there and read in the program that he had written it for her and dedicated it to her. Several hours after the concert, she sent him her thanks and congratulations. Despite the fact that he spoke little English, and she spoke almost no French at all, in no time they were a couple, then he proposed to her, and they were to be married! Both families were against the union, but his heart ruled his head, and they started a life together.

It was decided that they would live just outside Paris, in a rustic cottage (which is now the Ultrillo house in Montemarte). But it was not to be a happy situation for either of them. Her career was winding down, just as his was ramping up. She got pregnant, had a child, broke a leg, and stopped working. Meanwhile he became known as one of the great composers of his time. She grew to resent him tremendously. Jealousy and alcohol fueled her rage. The relationship went completely off the rails. He took on a mistress. She hired a lawyer. They parted ways forever shortly thereafter, and she died soon after that.

What started off as something amazing turned into a tragic union for all concerned. Both Hector and Harriet were diminished by having gotten together at all. Three plus three equaled negative five. Had he simply allowed the beautiful actress to be a point of inspiration, he might have written ten symphonies for her. But by trying to change the course of his destiny to include her life in his, he changed the course of his life in almost every other way. As fantastic as this story sounds, it's true.

The Wisdom—There is something to be said for knowing when to let a boyfriend or girlfriend simply be a boyfriend or girlfriend. There is great value in recognizing when a situation you are hoping to make happen may not survive all the effort required to make it happen. There is no need to fill the space between yourself and someone you think you have fallen in love with simply because you want to feel what everyone else is feeling. Mick Jagger once wrote, "Don't mortgage your soul to a stranger."

Not every romance should become a marriage. Not every time the words *I love you* are spoken should they be followed by the words *Will you marry me?* Sometimes enough is enough. Sometimes enough is too much. The recognition and acceptance of doubt is an important aspect of the decision-making process, especially where marriage and its consequences are concerned. *Oh, what the hell*, should not be the last thing you think before you say *I do*. You might save yourself a gruesome divorce by skipping over a bad marriage before it even happens.

Ten Years of Alimony, Five Years of Marriage

I direct your attention to the story of my dear friend Paul (not his real name either). He has been an extraordinary executive and creative force in the music business for at least two decades, now going on three. Everything he does, he does with oversize passion and zeal. You should hear him explain why one note out of place ruins an arrangement or why one word out of rhyme can ruin a lyric.

His first marriage was to a lovely young woman he met at the office. I attended the wedding. Because it was raining so hard that night, people were slipping and sliding around the church like keystone kops in films from long ago, and I saved an older man's life that evening when he tripped on a flight of stairs. But I am getting off the point. For whatever reason, Paul and Eunice could not figure out how to live together, at least not happily ever after. Married for just a few years, they made the decision to get a divorce. These few years in his life had been years of plenty, and lots of money came along with all that plenty. He was also a very generous man and wanted everyone to be happy, including his ex-wife and all the lawyers he was paying to represent her. So thinking that these good years would continue unabated for at least another decade or so, he agreed to a most generous settlement. Even though she had not worked even one afternoon while they were together, and even though he had worked his ass to the bone every day while they were together, he agreed to pay her more money than she had ever or would ever earn had she not been his wife. Mind you, he had paid for everything up to that point anyway, what with nice houses and nice cars and always flying in the front of the plane. Nonetheless, he agreed to further pay her $10,000 per month for the next ten years. Ten thousand dollars per month for ten years! That's $1.2 million. Just to say goodbye the right way?

You've got to admit, that is a lot of money. He could have easily made arguments that it should have been smaller payments for fewer years, but he would not make that particular argument. Crazy as it sounds, he believes he did the right thing. He has never looked back and never thought twice about how he handled it. He learned many lessons throughout their time together and gave her absolutely no reason whatsoever to disrespect or defame him, ever, for the rest of her life. And she never has. She remains his steadfast champion and has never said a word to the contrary about him. It was his decision to end the relationship, and it had less to do with her than you might think. He just wasn't happy. He knew that he needed to make some big changes. So he did. And did it right. And then what happened?

As soon as he was free, he went back in time and found the girl he was most in love with, way back when. She was the one he could never forget and the one who had haunted all his dreams. She was free, and he married her. Many years together and several children later, he will tell you he wouldn't change a thing about how everything went down. His ex-wife also came to realize they weren't meant to be together and cheers on his success and may be found occasionally at his house for a party. He got himself into the wrong situation and then got himself out of it, not blaming anyone but himself for the all the back and forth. He learned an expensive lesson and was happy to pay for his education.

The Wisdom—Money is money, but happiness is life. If you find yourself in the wrong house with the wrong husband or wife, extricate with kindness and generosity and move on with your world. And let him or her move on with theirs. Pay what you have to pay to make that happen and have a nice rest of your life.

CHAPTER 6

Divorcing and Children

No matter how children appear in your life, whether as your own, your new partner's, your grandchildren, or just a happy accident, they are yours now. They will look up to you. They will believe in you. They will trust you with their fragile hearts and big dreams. Protect them and defend them, especially in the event of a divorce.

The Calm and the Storm

Have you seen the movie *Life of Pi*? At the beginning, a little boy named Pi and some zoo animals are on a ship caught in a huge storm. Rain and thunder pour down out of the sky, as if from a fire hose. Huge waves crash on the weakened deck and set free every knot and every mooring, drowning most of the animals. And Pi's parents. It is a scene of such absolute chaos you can hardly breathe just watching it. When the storm is finally over, and the seas are calm again, Pi finds himself stranded, desperate, and alone in the middle of the ocean, in a rowboat, with a tiger. What a perfect analogy.

If you are not careful, that's what your divorce will be like for your children. Everything they know will be gone, everything they have learned to count on will have disappeared, and everything they ever wished for will have been washed away. And they will find themselves more alone more often than they have ever been before. You are both the calm and the storm. You are the source of their sadness, and you are the only one who can help them find their happiness again. They are looking to you for stability and purpose. They are seeking some kind of peace, and only you and your ex are the ones who can bring it to them.

Children's Needs Always Come First

---

1. *The Need to be Happy*—According to many studies on the subject, the children of divorce go to bed for many years of their lives hoping that their parents get back together. Even though the marriage has long since disappeared, and even when there are other partners involved, the dream remains. There is a disappointment that accompanies them the next morning when they realize that the dream did not come true, again. It is a sadness that will visit and revisit for years. Ah well. The counter to this weight is to truly celebrate your children every day. Be happy that they are with you. Recognize their accomplishments, their beauty, their grades, and the very fact of their existence, irrespective of the divorce and its aftermath. Even when they ask if you still love your ex—which they still do obviously—your answer has to be, "Yes, of course. How else would I know you?" Your happiness, whether real or imagined, will become their happiness. The more they feel happy around you, the sooner they will start to move past the sadness of the past.

2. *The Need to be Hopeful*—Children have simple systems to understand their own emotions and the

emotions of those around them. The world they inhabit is primary colors and primary emotions: red, blue, green, white; happy, sad, hopeful, disappointed. There is laughter, or there are tears. There is looking forward, or there is looking back. If their parents are getting a divorce, the children's sudden emotions brought about by the situation will not be nuanced or filtered. They will be brutally honest and forthright. Children display their emotions where everyone can see them. They keep their hearts on their sleeves because they have nowhere else to put them. Keeping the emotions of every day hopeful and positive is something they need to learn how to do. You can show them how. Again a simple solution—always looking forward to something. Maybe a trip or a party or a visit or a movie or something long planned that is finally happening. By letting them know that you are excited about the days ahead that you get to spend with them will provide a burst of hopefulness. Next visit, next week, next month, whatever and whenever. Always looking forward.

3. *The Need to be Blameless in the Divorce*—The promise of a forever family is one that you inherently made to your children. *We are together, and we will always be together* was an unwritten guarantee that they came to hope for and believe in. In a divorce, obviously that promise was broken. A new reality has come to be. The family they had come to expect, and believe in, is no more. A life they

dared to dream of has disappeared. And who is to blame for this? Is it your children? No, not at all. It cannot ever be the children's fault. They are innocent. They are refugees from the land of dreams. No part of the divorce can be because of them. The divorce cannot have happened because of anything they did or said. You must never infer or suggest otherwise. You got a divorce. You did not divorce your children. Your children were just passengers on the trip. Their heads are filled with questions, and most of them have no right answers.

But all the research indicates that they will blame themselves anyway, regardless of what you say about it. If you are not sensitive to their feelings of guilt, it will turn into something much worse and long lasting. Things happen. Divorces happen. Your children are not responsible for it and must hear that from you. Blameless is a feeling that every divorced child deserves to know. Save them from years of guilt and therapy to assuage that guilt by letting them know it has nothing to do with them. Let them know too that there is still a family, and that family will always be, even if it is now living in separate houses.

4. *The Need to Love Themselves and Who They Are*— When a divorce is underway, the parents often feel that they can share their petty dislikes and annoyances and grievances about the former spouse with the children. But for all you may know, a particular habit may be part of why your children love the

other parent so much. Maybe your ex's forgetfulness endears her to the children, even though you always felt slighted when she never remembered your wedding anniversary. Maybe their father was a bit of a slob and never cleaned up the house. It could be that your children love the fact that their dad is not the perfect housekeeper because they can relax around him. But wait. Children know that they have traits from both sides, that they are like both of you in some ways or even in many ways. They know they are a jigsaw puzzle made up of little pieces of the parents, the grandparents, and all the other antecedents. They see themselves in their relatives.

So while you may think you are just criticizing your former spouse or the family, what you are actually doing is criticizing your child. And the more you invest in the criticism, the more the child will see themselves in the words you are using. Repeatedly paint an unflattering portrait of your spouse and the family, and your children will only see themselves in the final rendering. And ultimately your children may come to feel that there is less to like about themselves. Which just *cannot* happen. Love your children without any criticisms directed at them or their relatives, and they might just love themselves that way too.

Be the Best Listener Ever

So how do you inspire your children's faith in you again? How do you start all over at being the best parent in the world? How do you win their hearts back? To me, with my two boys, I started with a simple gift. I gave them this gift whenever we were together. I listened. And listened and listened. Not only to the things they were saying, but also to the things they were not saying because they didn't know how. I heard the sadness and the disappointment that bloomed because their mother and I were not a couple any longer, because I no longer lived in the same house with them. I did not pretend that everything was fine every minute. I did not shut them up or shut them down. I let them talk. I listened for the emotions. I savored the details.

And if you're in this same situation where your kids are unsure of their futures and afraid of their pasts, it's what you will need to do. You will need to listen to them. And listen. And listen. Be the best listener your children have ever known. Be a legendary listener. Even their stories about your ex and how she is doing without you. Or a story of a dinner you were not invited to. Or a party you missed. Even if it kills you inside. Even if you are dying, story by story. Even if your regrets outlast your patience. Laugh when they laugh, cry when they cry. It's part of the mosaic of proof that you are the best parent ever.

Your children are adjusting to a new universe. You are not the same person who used to be right down the hall when they woke up. Now they need to find a phone if they want to talk with you. Or wait for the next scheduled visit. All that said, you can still be the one to help them find peace. You can still be the kindest one in their rocky world. It's not that hard to do. Just hear what they have to say. Pay close attention and look them in the eye as they speak. There is no such a thing as multitasking when you are talking to your kids. So no multitasking. No e-mails or texting while talking. Just let it be you and your children. Whether in a phone call, in person, Skype, Zoom, whatever. Be the best listener.

Your instinct meanwhile will be telling you to talk more and make them listen to you more. This will happen because you don't have as much time as you used to have with them. Visits will be on the clock in some respects. And you will have a lot to say to them. And a lot less time to say it. Override the urge to share every idea that crosses your mind. Skip some of your wisdom till the next visit. Listen more than you talk. Listen. Listen. Listen. You will get more out of your time with your children.

Gift-Giving

Let's discuss this. Your children must continue to have and know the joy of giving the other parent gifts and recognizing how great a parent he or she is. Mother's Day. Father's Day. Birthdays. Holidays. All of 'em. But wait. Where are they going to find the money for such things, you ask? That's right. You. Even though it's your ex, you must continue to finance the children's adulation of the other parent.

As discussed previously, generosity is the foundation of a good divorce. And facilitating your children's gift giving to the other parent (i.e., your ex) falls into that same category. It's just one of those things. Please don't throw the book across the room. Consider it like this, financing your children's generosity to the other parent is a sign of your maturity and ability to move forward with your life despite the many challenges. It shows the world, and your kids, what a good person you are, were, and always will be. It is the kind of thing that will continue to preserve your good divorce.

Will and His Son Harry

It's not just the parents who go through the divorce, it's the children too. Their lives are the ones that are turned around and upside down, tossed in the air to land on the hard ground. At least the parents have some way to prepare themselves for all of the insanity based on some previous life experiences, or books like this one, or hearing the stories of other survivors. But kids do not have that deep a pool in which to cast themselves. In many ways, they are defenseless. Defenseless kids will often say things that are true at that specific moment but not true for a lifetime, or probably not even true later that same day. They will blurt out their thoughts. They will say things that probably should not be said. They are more anxious than they have ever been. They may not even know that they are going over the line. But their emotions take over, and the words come out. This is the story of one of those situations.

In the middle of his divorce, Will was trying to do right by everyone. He got the wife and kids a house of their own, moved into an apartment down the street, and agreed to pay for everything. He just did not want to be married to his wife any longer. Of course the kids felt that what he was really saying was that he did not want to be married to *them* any longer. They were hurt. They were unsure. They were positive of only one thing, and that was that their mother had been wronged, and they had been wronged too. So at some point, Will's then-fourteen-year-old son Harry turned to him and said something along the lines of, "I hate you. I hate what you've done to our family. I hope I never see you again."

Little did the boy know that his father was still a child inside. A hurt and angry child whose own father had left him standing at a doorstep, in the middle of the Depression, with nothing but a goodbye. Will's father had walked out on his family that day and was never seen again. He left Will, his three siblings, and their mother to fend for themselves. Turned out he was a terrible alcoholic who would die a few years later, drowned and facedown in two inches of water. Alcoholism was and is a terrible disease, little known at that time. Little did the son know that Will was never able to recover from his own terrible injury or that it was permanent or that it was the cause of anger and pain and sadness from which there was no relief to be found.

Will's son was just a kid mouthing off to his father, a father who had just divorced his mom. He was angry and being rude and touching the edges of the new boundaries that the divorce had just put in place. But what Harry could never know was that his father, a child himself in so many ways, would take him at his word, literally and figuratively. *Will never spoke to his son again, ever.* He sent checks to cover the bills and schools and sports, sent everyone on vacations and trips, but never again did he say a word to his own son. Never. He did to his son what had been done to him.

Instead of doing everything in his power to make his child's life better than his own, and his child's journey somehow smoother and easier than his own had been, Will took the exact opposite path. He tried to ruin his son's life just the same way that his own life had been ruined. He tried to hurt him the way he had been hurt. He tried to punish him the way he had been punished. I only found this all out after Will passed away, and I called his son to offer my condolences.

Harry said, "Thanks for calling, but I haven't spoken to my dad in almost twenty-five years."

When I asked why, out came this story. More awful still was the fact that Will was a father figure to many other people, including me and my brother, and other nieces and nephews in the family and the employees that worked for him, and on and on. But he could never forgive his own son for one thoughtless remark. Never got over it. Missed out on hundreds of conversations, experiences, laughs, trips, and a wedding even, any one of which might have healed him, or at least started the healing process. And it was basically over nothing!

During your divorce, chances are that your children will be hit the hardest of all the participants. They will be the ones most shocked and traumatized by the new world order you've just thrown at them. They will lose their sense of right and wrong at some point and will forget their boundaries, and just may blurt out something terrible to you or your ex or about you to your ex, or something like that. You have a couple of choices when it happens. You can be Will and use the rest of your life to retaliate and miss out on your child's life, or you can rise above it and forgive. I recommend the forgiving.

The children of divorce are so vulnerable! When the divorce crashes on the beaches of their lives, it will wipe out everything they have known and have been sure of, just like the opening of *Pi*. It is that devastating to them, and the only person who can understand it is you, the person responsible for it. If they say something awful, let it be a moment in time that comes and goes. If they revolt and break some new rules you've set down, let it be something you choose to understand rather than something you choose to let ruin everything that came before and everything that will come after. If they do not listen to you, try to listen to them even more. Maybe they are trying to tell you something. If they lose interest in you, do everything you can to be more interested in them and more interesting to them. Even if they say the unforgivable, forgive them anyway. In time, they will come to understand how hard you have tried to keep them close to you.

Roles Your Children Can Play in a Good Divorce

Anyone with a heart knows that a good life for the children in a divorce is a forever goal that must always be pursued. Their hopeful hearts are fragile. Their ability to understand why and how things happened the way they happened is limited. But preserving their innocence is one of the most important jobs you have as a divorced parent. There are several ways your children can play a part in your divorced life and, at the same time, help themselves survive this whole thing.

1. *Sources of good advice.* They have a tendency to speak the truth about things even when they might not understand all the details. Keep listening to what they suggest and offer. Kids say the darndest things.

2. *Constant reminders of why you are here.* Your kids will love you forever if you give them the slightest reason to do so. They are your legacy, after all, and your inspiration and your hope for a better future. That's why you had them, right?

3. *Believers in your goodness.* You don't divorce your kids, even if it feels that way a little bit. They are sympathetic to your situation. They see that you are changed by it. They want to help you through

all of it. By showing them your kindness and your patience, you will be showing them your goodness too. Give them every reason to still believe in your kind heart.

4. *Inaccurate historians.* Your children have short memories and want to love you, regardless of what happened. They do not carry around all the same baggage your ex does—thank goodness—and are quite willing to forget the bad and welcome the good. Every day is a chance to start all over again, just like in *50 First Dates.*

5. *Your best pals.* Now that you don't have to worry about the other parent when you're with your kids, there will be many more chances to just hang around with them, knock about, and waste a little time, doing little or doing nothing if you want. You can take them anywhere. Movies, golf, dinner, walks. They can help run errands, clean up the house, challenge you at video games. Every moment does not have to be a teaching moment. Maybe chill out a little and enjoy the time with them more.

6. *Partners in laughter.* One of most children's favorite things to do is have a good laugh. And you cannot let them forget how to do this. It is good for them to do and good for you too. Search out funny. In anything and everywhere. Get the first real laugh of the day for everyone by noon if at all possible. Whatever is funny, pursue it! *New Yorker* cartoons, *Far Side* compendiums, *Saturday Night Live* skits,

YouTube cute puppy videos, Howard Stern inter-
views, Bugs Bunny quotes, Instagram or TikTok
memes, whatever it takes. Laughing is healthy! Like
Keto. And kale.

"That Woman"

When you are writing a book, you end up living it, thinking it, falling asleep with it, talking about it all the time, and even dreaming about how to say something so perfectly that it will make perfect sense to a thousand strangers who might read your book someday. And so it happened that I was walking on a beach near my house last year and ran into a man and his family. He seemed like a nice-enough guy, had two great kids, a lovely wife, all of them out enjoying a day in the sun. We got to talking, and when he asked what I did with my time, I mentioned that I was writing this book, my fifth, and that it was a book about divorce, and my take on how to achieve the wonders of a good divorce. That it was written in the hopes of giving people the tools and plans to help them achieve the wonder of a good divorce.

He shook his head from side to side, let out sort of a low noise, and said, "I wish my dad had read a book like that, I really do…"

I started questioning him, softly digging in and around and trying to understand why that was his reaction. He told me that his parents divorced when he was still in single digits, like seven or eight or something like that. There was enough money around so that no one was living in poverty, but it took a little while for his dad to get back on his feet and find some sort of happiness again. But then he went on to tell me how his dad never got over the fact of the divorce or that the marriage had come to an end. His father refused to come into the old house. He would not sit with his ex at their children's music recitals or sporting events. He would not send her holiday cards and would throw away the ones she sent him, even though they had pictures of his own children on the front. He would not visit his children on Thanksgiving if the ex was going to be there at the celebration. The very idea of her, or anything to do with her, actually repulsed him. And then the son told me how his father referred to his mother. Even thirty years later, he still called her "that woman."

Because the father was unable to reconcile his future with his past, everyone else in his family had to accommodate him and his insecurities. Not only were all the holidays bifurcated by the fact that the father was inflexible and unforgiving, so too were the weddings, baptisms, christenings—in fact, every family event. And all of this nonsense just because they got a divorce? I ascertained that the wife had done nothing of note and had not embarrassed her husband or family in any way. She simply wanted out of the marriage. Apparently enough was enough. And if he was like this during the divorce and its aftermath, can you imagine how much fun he was to be around during the marriage? *No wonder she left him*, I thought. He sounded like a real piece of work. Not that I said that to the man on the beach that day.

The man, a victim of his parents' divorce as much as anything else, was still sad about the whole thing and carried it around with him. He was saddled with his father's old luggage and broken dreams. He felt terrible for his mom, who was still being punished for the rest of her life by her ex-husband. He shook his head from side to side and said again, "I wish my dad had read a book about how to get divorced. It would have made life so much easier for everybody."

There is no reason why your children should ever have to tell a story like this one about you or your spouse. There is no reason why you should be grumpy and stay grumpy for the rest of your life. There is no reason why you need to punish anyone simply because the marriage ended. Marriages end. Get over it. It was never more than a fifty-fifty bet in the first place. Your children have done absolutely nothing to deserve any negative feelings from you. They were along for the ride; they didn't choose the ride. They will have done nothing to deserve even an ounce of your resentment, should any be lingering. They are, first and always, your purpose for being here. Love them. Respect them. Be kind to them. Don't make them suffer because you want to suffer. Your divorce was yours. It is your problem, not theirs.

The Longer-Term Effects of Divorce on Children and Ways to Combat Them

There have been many studies on the effect of divorce on children. The studies show that the lives of children of divorce are unquestionably impacted by the fact that the parents were unable to stay together. Most children think their parents are great at everything and can solve every single problem, and this image is shattered by a divorce. These same children then begin to walk into their futures with some doubts about their own ability to fall in love and sustain a relationship. They wonder if they can solve problems without things blowing up in their faces. They live with nagging questions about their own invincibility, especially where love is concerned. Many see this doubt manifest as an overall pessimism that pervades their lives, leading to a measurable loss of self-confidence. They also begin to see divorce or breaking up as an option in any situation. You have to do everything in your power to prevent these kinds of negative thoughts from finding a home in their hearts.

Knowing that the divorce was going to be very tough for my boys, no matter what, I did everything in my power to make sure that they were not suffocated by all the circumstances that were about to engulf them. I did whatever I could to allow them to have a chance at a beautiful future, regardless of how the divorce might have, in any way, diminished those chances. I did not want them to be overwhelmed by the breakup of their mother and me and gave them every opportunity to achieve some normalcy in their lives.

These were my strategies to achieve all this:

1. I did not suddenly divorce their mother. It didn't come out of nowhere. I had let them know that there were struggles and that their mom and I were doing everything we could to work them out.

2. Once divorced, I purposely waited a very long time to have another child, almost ten years in fact, and this gave both of my first boys a chance to have their whole childhood with me and without the distractions of a younger needier person in the mix.

3. Once my new son arrived, I gave his two older brothers the responsibility of naming their younger brother. This was a way of joining them at the hip, making them closer to one another rather than separating them and making one jealous of the other in any way.

4. I continued to coach, mentor, chauffer, launder, sometimes cook, and visit almost every single day with both older boys, ensuring that there was no time difference in the time commitment between me the dad who lived with them and me the dad who did not any longer.

5. I made sure to never speak to my ex through my children and never let them know of any displeasure or unhappiness I might be feeling about her

at any particular time. As far as they knew, things were always perfect, it was just that we weren't married anymore.

6. I never forced my new son on the older boys and have let them discover each other pretty much at their own pace. And they are all now good pals.

7. I was always available to converse, eat, play, read, practice, whatever. We continued our yearly ski trip tradition without a break as well.

Please be aware that your search for a new happiness (and a new spouse maybe) should not come at the cost of your children pursuing their own wonderful lives. Yes, go find the next perfect person in your life, and good luck! But try not to do this at the expense of your children's dreams and hopes for their future. They should grow up believing that a great marriage is possible and that it just might happen for them. This is irrespective of what may or may not have happened to you.

Rights I Gave My Kids

In addition to the gift of listening to them, I also gave my two older sons a slate of rights once I was divorced from their mother. These were meant to be like a passport to privileges that would protect them and their hearts in the aftermath of the divorce. All were born from my desire to not diminish either of their lives in any way simply because their mother and I were no longer a married couple.

Whenever I was with them, I reminded myself to adhere to the power of these entitlements, whether during a meal, a conversation, a drive, a sleepover, a phone call, or whatever the interaction was. These rights overrode all others. I cannot say it was always perfect, but I was trying to reduce their sadness and reimagine their happiness every time we were together. For their part, the boys have turned out to be wonderful men, and I think they fully understand it was about me and their mother, not them.

These are the rights I gave them:

1. The right to speak to me about everything and anything. If it crossed one of their minds, they could open up their hearts without fear of being rejected or rushed, even if what they had to say was hard for me to hear.

2. The right to be loving toward their mom and appreciative of her many gifts, without worrying if that would hurt my feelings somehow.

3. The right to my complete respect. I had always been kindhearted and gentle toward them, but once divorced, I doubled down and made sure they always knew that my first and always priority was them. I listened when they spoke. I paid attention. I looked them in the eye. I respected them in every way I could imagine.

4. The right to celebrate the lives and family we had before the divorce came along and took all that away. Meaning that they could watch old home movies and leaf through the photo albums and reminisce about the many good times we had before.

5. The right to make suggestions to me on any subject, including telling me when I was absolutely and completely wrong about something. This included being able to disagree about some plans I had made for an afternoon or a weekend without it being seen as an act of treason.

6. The right to start any conversation over. This is such an important privilege to give your child or children. For our family interactions, any talk on any subject, at any time, either one could raise his hand and say, "Let's start this conversation over, please." So if the exchange of ideas was turning into a disagreement or otherwise not turning out like either one wanted it to be, they could always hit the reset button.

CHAPTER 7

Final Thoughts

This Whole Book in One Page

Kindness. Respect. Generosity. These are the goals to guide your actions and behavior and the key ingredients of your good divorce.

Give the marriage every chance, then break up right. These are two things you do to ensure that you and your spouse are positioned to start and finish as partners, giving you both a chance at a good divorce.

Let the lawyer be the lawyer and keep your emotions under control. This will allow the legal machinations of your divorce to proceed without disruptions, interruptions, or vitriol.

Avoid arguments, and try to say nothing critical. These are guardrails that will keep your situation from getting out of control, while providing you with a passport to a great life during and after your good divorce.

Life Is What Happens

You didn't plan on getting a divorce, and you probably always hoped you would never become one of the statistics that defines this age. But here you are, divorced. And now suppose you suddenly find yourself with a chance at a new relationship. All your friends have been making suggestions and inviting you to awkward get-togethers, and someone finally starts to make sense. Or maybe your efforts on e-harmony actually introduce you to someone that fits your new life. Or you bump into someone at a Starbucks and see your future in the way they smile at you. But then suppose it is sooner than you expected, and you're just not ready, still unsure of your new footing, hardly prepared to love again. Suppose, suppose, suppose.

Once married and divorced, the statistics suggest that most people will probably get married again, and some of them again and again until they get it right. A new connection is a form of reincarnation. A new wife is a chance at a new life. A new husband is a chance for a new and different future. Happiness is out there somewhere, if you could only find a place for yourself in someone else's heart. This new person, whoever they might be, has to be able to find you too by the way. Which means you have to get your ass off the sofa, back to the gym, and back into the game. Life will be going forward, whether you like it or not, with or without your willing participation. Life is what happens! Whether meeting a beautiful person in a rainstorm like I was lucky enough to do, or anywhere else, under any other circumstances, you have to be ready. My father used to say that opportunity has only one hair on his head, and you have to yank it out as he walks by. Or else watch him walk down the street and see someone else grab on to it.

Life is not what you expected, as your divorce has shown you. And now that you know that, you have to be prepared for anything and everything that might be coming at you. Life is going to keep happening, whether you're ready or not.

If Your New Love Doesn't Want the Ex Around, That's It!

My wife allows me to be friends with my ex. The operating word here is *allows*. Not a lot of women would, I imagine, but this one is very smart about such things. She knows me and knows I have no interest in rekindling anything, and that goes double for my ex. My ex knew me when and has no interest in knowing me now. Older, heavier, hairier. My wife also knows that women almost never go back. Ever. Over is over. Done is done. So there are no worries. And this friendship with my ex has been good for me, my sons, all the in-laws, and everyone else involved, whether intimately or tangentially. It's healthy and positive to see a divorce work as well as ours does. And I am so incredibly grateful to my wife for it. It is a gift she gives me every day. But I think she also knows that if she didn't want it to happen, it wouldn't happen.

Your Relationship with Your Ex Isn't Over

The relationship has not ended just because of the divorce.

It's not over, it's just different. It has evolved. Maybe what that new metric is isn't clear yet, but the relationship absolutely still exists. You will have to still talk to each other about something or other all the time. About taxes, money, investments, things you bought and own together, stocks and bonds, school recitals, tuition for the kids, whatever. Just because the marriage is over does not mean that the relationship is over. You don't have to sell the restaurant or the boat or the place in Mammoth just because you are divorcing.

As time progresses, you will fall in love with someone else, as will your ex. You might even get married again, who knows. Lots of people do. There will be weddings to attend and graduations and baptisms and soccer games and so on. There will be lots of ways to interact and stay involved in each other's lives. Let the new relationship evolve at its own pace and tempo. No need to rush anything.

You Don't Really Win a Divorce

You don't win a divorce, you get through it. And if you follow even half of the guidelines laid out here, you will survive it and thrive afterward.

The divorce is a rite of passage between your past and your future. Handle it with grace and do the right things, and you can sail into your tomorrows with no regrets to hold you back. Perhaps your spouse gets a little more of something. Maybe it's money or time with the kids or the right to half your Nobel Prize money, but so what? The past is the past and the future is everything. You will have earned the freedom to walk away and start all over. Don't worry about who won.

All My Wives Have Ocean Views

I might have mentioned that my new family and my old family live just a few blocks apart, all of us close enough to the coast to see the water. And for good reason. I wanted it this way. I wanted everyone happy. Kids, wife, ex-wife, everybody. I knew the divorce had to be good for both sides if it was to be a good divorce, and I did everything within my power to make sure that happened. The long-term and long-lasting effect of those efforts has been remarkable. My ex-mother-in-law is my real estate agent. My ex-brother-in-law, the doctor, literally saved my life with his treatment of my awful disease. My ex-wife cheers me on and has never said a bad word about me to anyone. Not even one friend had to choose which side of the divorce to be on. Even my ex-sister-in-law's father, who lives just down the street is a pal. There has been no resentment and no griping by anyone involved in the divorce because there was no reason.

Since my own divorce, I have mentored and coached four men into good divorces. Using most—if not all—of the ideas in here, they split up with their wives (one with his husband) without rancor or sorrow. They only wrote one or two checks instead of a lifetime of them. They have established complementary lives with their exes and all the other family members involved. They are, most importantly, actively part of their children's lives and stayed friends with most of the friends they enjoyed during the marriage. The divorce didn't destroy them and it didn't really diminish them all that much either. I expect there will be more. I expect that I will be there for any and every one of my pals, male or female, who exhaust all other options in their marriages and see a divorce as the only way forward.

What has this taught me? It has taught me that it is possible to end a marriage without ending a life. It has taught me that it is feasible to say goodbye to one kind of relationship with a spouse and say hello to another. It has taught me that it is reasonable to expect a good outcome if one shows respect, kindness, and generosity before, during, and after the divorce.

By ensuring that both of the women who married me still have plenty of reasons to love me, I have given myself a passport to real and forever happiness. And they both got fabulous ocean views.

ACKNOWLEDGMENTS AND THANK-YOU'S

Thank you, first and always, to my amazing wife, who allows me to have a great friendship with my ex and supports every effort I make to write the perfect book.

Thank you to my ex for our good divorce and the lifetime friendship that has followed on from it.

Thank you to my three sons, who provide me with constant inspiration to get along with everyone.

Thank you to Mike Schiff for the foreword and also for handling my divorce.

Thank you to many friends who read through various versions of the manuscript and gave comments and suggestions, particularly Lou Arnell, Bob Davis, Miles King, Scott Tobis, D. Kern Holoman, and Catherine Wyler.

Thank you to Larry King, a man who knew a great deal about divorce. We talked about the idea for this book at Clive Davis' Grammy Party in 2019. After I told him what I was trying to do, he tapped me on the forearm and said, "It will be a very important book." His words inspired me to keep at it.

Thank you to Clive Davis. When I told him what was happening in my marriage and how it was killing me to be in a divorce, he said "You have the right to be happy." I have lived by his wisdom ever since.

Lastly, thank you to Michael Rosen, who lost his fight with pancreatic cancer this year. He was my mentor through my divorce, as well as my secret weapon and confidante. He was the guy who told me to just keep my mouth shut and write one check. His wisdom is everywhere in this book.

Love you Mike and miss you every day.

APPENDIX 1

Some songs I pitched and the artists who recorded them:

"We Belong" (Eric Lowen/Dan Navarro)
Pat Benatar

"Heart of Stone" (Andy Hill/Pete Sinfield)
Cher

"Think Twice" (Andy Hill/Pete Sinfield)
Celine Dion

"Every Time You Go Away" (Darryl Hall)
Paul Young (shared credit)

"An Angel Cries" (Simon Climie/Dennis Morgan)
Aretha Franklin

"I Knew You Were Waiting for Me" (Simon Climie/Dennis Morgan)
Aretha Franklin and George Michael

"Always Drive A Cadillac" (Larry Raspberry)
The Everly Brothers

"Tired of Being Blonde" (Larry Raspberry)
Carly Simon

"If It Takes All Night" (David Bryant/Jay Gruska)
Janet Jackson

"Another Life" (P.G. Sturges/Andy Hill)
Barry Manilow

"The Face In The Window" (Eric Lowen/Dan Navarro/Rick Boston)
Nile Rodgers

"When The Radio is On" (Matt Noble/Kevin Hazlett)
Paul Schaffer

"Wait For Me" (Antonina Armato/Rick Neigher)
Taylor Dayne

"If" (David Gates)
Julio Iglesias

"I Still Believe" (Antonina Armato/Beppe Cantorelli)
Mariah Carey

APPENDIX 2

Some of the artists, producers and songwriters I signed to music publishing deals:

Red Hot Chili Peppers
Katrina and the Waves
Smashing Pumpkins
Vinnie Vincent Invasion
Slaughter
Billy Burnette
Steve Cropper
Andy Hill
Shaquille O'Neal
Antonina Armato
3 Doors Down
Foo Fighters
Jack Johnson
Chris Brown
50 Cent
Afroman
Mark Batson

Jason Epperson aka Jay E
Owl City
Vanessa Carlton
Baby Bash
Outkast and Goodie Mob
Rock Mafia
Montell Jordan
Childish Gambino
Billy Bizeau
Kipper Jones
Eric Lowen & Dan Navarro
P.G. Sturges
Andy Hill
Larry Raspberry
Stone Temple Pilots
Simon Climie

Although I did not sign the following artist/writers, I had the privilege of working with them as their music publisher: Paul Anka, Billy Idol, Bon Jovi, U2, Carole King, Sinead O'Connor, Beastie Boys, Richie Sambora, Jethro Tull, Gerry Goffin, and Pat Benatar.

OTHER BOOKS BY TOM STURGES

Parking Lot Rules & Other Ideas for Raising Amazing Children
(Ballantine Books-Random House, 2008)

Grow the Tree You Got & Other Ideas for Raising Amazing Adolescents and Teenagers
(Tarcher Penguin-Random House, 2011)

Every Idea Is a Good Idea: Be Creative Anytime, Anywhere
(Tarcher Penguin-Random House, 2014)

Preston Sturges: The Last Years of Hollywood's First Writer-Director
(Intellect-University of Chicago Press, 2019)